Dundon's

Modern
IRISH
FOOD

More than 100 recipes
for easy comfort food

Kevin Dundon's

Modern IRISH FOOD

More than 100 recipes
for easy comfort food

MITCHELL BEAZLEY

An Hachette UK Company
www.hachette.co.uk

First published in Great Britain in 2013
by Mitchell Beazley, a division of
Octopus Publishing Group Ltd,
Carmelite House,
50 Victoria Embankment,
London EC4Y 0DZ
www.octopusbooks.co.uk
www.octopusbooksusa.com

First published in paperback in 2016

Distributed in the US by
Hachette Book Group
1290 Avenue of the Americas
4th and 5th Floors
New York, NY 10020

Distributed in Canada by
Canadian Manda Group
664 Annette Street
Toronto, Ontario, Canada M6S 2C8

ISBN 978-1-78472-245-6

A CIP catalogue record for this book is available
from the British Library

Set in Georgia PS

Printed and bound in China

10 9 8 7 6 5 4 3 2 1

Group Publishing Director: Denise Bates
Managing Editor: Clare Churly
Senior Art Editor: Juliette Norsworthy
Home Economist: Kate Blinman
Stylist: Jessica Georgiades
Photographer: Cristian Barnett
Production Manager: Caroline Alberti

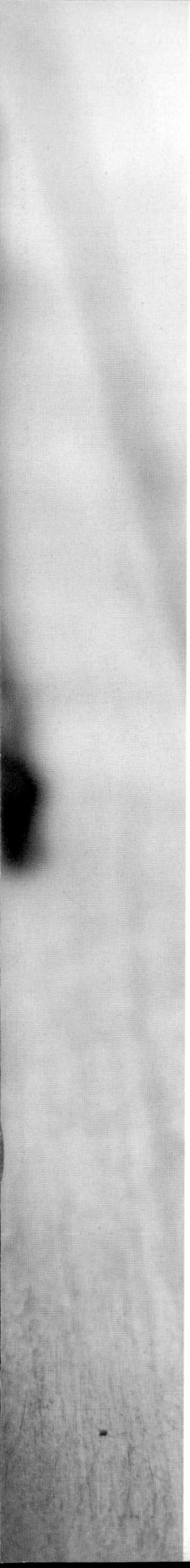

Contents

Introduction   6

Soups   8

Breads   26

Fish and Seafood   40

Poultry and Game   66

Meat   90

Vegetarian   124

Salads and Side Dishes   138

Something Sweet   168

Storecupboard, Sauces and Stocks   202

Index   220

Acknowledgements   224

This book has been inspired by my love of food and, specifically, of locally sourced, seasonal, good-quality, fresh Irish food. I believe Irish food is worth celebrating, and in Ireland that means being with family and friends in the kitchen, which was, and still is, the heart of every Irish home.

For me it is Irish food all the way! But the world is a great melting pot of culinary traditions, tastes and experiences, and throughout my career I have been lucky enough to travel extensively and enjoy foods from many parts of the world. So in this book, while I have used mostly traditional ingredients, I could not resist adding a twist here and there, pulling in ingredients and cooking techniques from other cultures in a way that simply combines great foods.

Irish food remains predominately traditional because recipes have been handed down along the generations. In my case, recipes were passed to me by my grandmother and mother, both of whom have inspired my passion for cooking. Irish food is often thought to consist of nothing but stews and potatoes. While these are important elements of our heritage, our cuisine is made up of far more than just these things. We draw on the wealth of ingredients available on our doorstep, from beef that has grazed on lush pasturelands, and sheep and lamb that feed on heathers growing on our rugged mountains, to the sweet, delicate seafood from the seas that surround our beautiful country.

There is something unique in every county in Ireland that gives Irish food a strong personality –

Introduction

of both the place and its producers. The list of beautifully crafted Irish cheeses is a prime example of this, with such fantastic products as Durrus, Cashel Blue, St Tola, Knockdrinna, Milleen and Cooleeney, to mention just a few. The same can be said of producers of other products, from yogurts, butters and creams to meat, poultry and condiments.

In our kitchen at Dunbrody Country House Hotel, we are lucky enough to have these wonderful products at our disposal. We like to think that we take good products and combine them into something even better. I hope that this book allows you, time and time again, to take a recipe and some good ingredients that I recommend, or similar products from producers local to you,

and turn them into a restaurant-quality dish to share with your family and friends.

This book was written at Dunbrody Country House Hotel, which is where I live and work. This award-winning hotel and restaurant, located on the Hook Peninsula in County Wexford, retains an old world charm and elegance that we like to emulate in the restaurant. Dunbrody House, as well as the Raglan Road Irish Gastropub in Orlando, Florida, for which I also design menus and recipes as chef-partner, allow me to put into practice my ethos for using locally sourced, seasonal food. I hope you enjoy them as much as our guests do.

Happy cooking!

Kevin

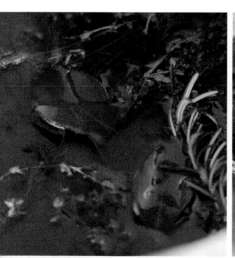

Soups

Just a small portion of this soup will be enough – it is a delicious
way to begin a dinner party. Sometimes I use smoked bacon
or wild garlic instead of fresh mint to flavour the soup.

SERVES 6

25g (2 tbsp) butter
1 large onion, chopped
2 garlic cloves, chopped
1 potato, cut into small pieces
450g (3 cups) fresh or frozen peas
Salt and black pepper
700ml (3 cups) chicken or
   vegetable stock
125ml (½ cup) pouring (light) cream
2 tbsp chopped mint

Garden Pea and Mint Soup

Put the butter into a saucepan and sauté the onion, garlic and potato until
lightly browned.

Throw the peas into the pot and mix them around for a moment until they
are lightly glazed with the butter mixture. Add in a pinch of salt and a crack
of black pepper.

Next, pour in the chicken stock and pouring cream and bring the mixture
to a rapid boil. Reduce the heat and simmer for 10–12 minutes until the peas
have softened, yet still retain their green colour. Add in the mint and mix well.

Blitz the mixture to a smooth consistency using a handheld blender or a food
processor (in batches if necessary).

Return the soup to the heat, adjust the seasoning and reheat gently. Serve
immediately with some crusty bread.

Although I have used spring cabbage in this recipe, you can use whatever cabbage is in season.

SERVES 4

1kg (2¼lb) young spring cabbage
    (or 1 large head)
2 litres (8½ cups) light chicken stock
    or ham stock
Salt and black pepper
2 carrots, chopped
6 small leeks, trimmed and thinly sliced
2 garlic cloves, crushed
600g (1¼lb) potatoes (or 5 potatoes),
    cut into small pieces
1 bay leaf
1 sprig of thyme
50g (4 tbsp) butter

Spring Cabbage Soup

First, cut out the central core and stems of the cabbage leaves. Set aside.

Pour the stock into a large saucepan, bring it to the boil, then add the cabbage leaves and blanch for 2 minutes. Remove the leaves from the stock and set aside.

Season the stock with salt and black pepper, then add the carrots, leeks, garlic, potatoes and herbs. Bring to the boil, then reduce the heat and simmer for 30–40 minutes until the carrots and potatoes are softened.

Add the blanched cabbage and blitz the mixture to a smooth consistency using a handheld blender or a food processor (in batches if necessary).

Return the soup to the heat and finish by adding the butter gradually, which gives the soup a lovely gloss. Serve immediately.

This is a really nice, simple soup to make because it requires so few ingredients. You should, however, try to obtain a flavoursome beef stock, because this enhances the flavour of the soup. It is particularly tasty if made the day before serving, which allows time for the flavours to develop. Reheat it slowly to serve.

SERVES 6

115g (1 stick) butter
4 large onions, thinly sliced
3 garlic cloves
1 tsp crushed black pepper
2–3 sprigs of thyme
2 tsp demerara sugar or other raw sugar
300ml (1¼ cups) white wine
1 litre (4¼ cups) warm beef or chicken
    stock

FOR THE CHEESY CROUTONS
1 stick or loaf of French bread
3 tbsp olive oil
50g (½ cup) Parmesan or Gruyère
    cheese, grated

Caramelized Onion Soup with Cheesy Croutons

Preheat the oven to 180°C/350°F/gas mark 4.

In a large saucepan, melt the butter and carefully add in the onion, garlic, black pepper and thyme sprigs. Sweat off the onion over a medium heat for about 10 minutes or until it has partially softened, turned brown and caramelized.

Add in the demerara sugar and allow it to melt completely and infuse the onion.

Pour in the wine and gradually add the stock, stirring slowly. Bring to the boil, then reduce the heat and simmer for about 45 minutes or until the onion is soft and the soup is highly flavoured.

Meanwhile, make the croutons. Cut the French bread into slices about 1cm (½in) thick and drizzle with olive oil. Place on a baking sheet and bake in the oven for 6 minutes. Sprinkle with the grated cheese, then return to the oven for another 4 minutes until the cheese is melted.

Pour the fragrant soup into serving bowls, top each portion with some croutons and serve immediately.

If you have too many cherry tomatoes in the garden, or surplus fruit from other recipes, freezing them is a good option. You can then use them for making soup instead of seeing them all go to waste. Garlic chives are similar to ordinary chives but have a faint garlic flavour.

SERVES 6

2 tbsp olive oil
1 small onion, finely chopped
3 garlic cloves, roasted (see box)
1kg (2¼lb) ripe cherry tomatoes, halved
1 handful of garlic chives (or use regular chives), chopped

700ml (3 cups) warm light chicken stock or water
2 potatoes, cut into small pieces
Salt and black pepper
Pinch of light brown sugar
200ml (1 cup) pouring (light) cream

Cherry Tomato and Roasted Garlic Soup

Heat the olive oil in a saucepan over a medium-high heat. Add the onion and squeeze in the pulp from the roasted garlic cloves. Sauté for 2–3 minutes until golden.

Add the cherry tomatoes and continue to sauté for a further 3–4 minutes until the mixture is heated through and just beginning to break down.

Add in half the garlic chives. Stir in the chicken stock or water and allow the mixture to come to the boil, then add the potatoes. Reduce the heat and simmer for about 20 minutes until everything has softened.

Blitz the mixture to a smooth consistency using a handheld blender or a food processor (in batches if necessary). Return the soup to the heat, season with salt and pepper to taste (the soup will take quite a lot of cracked black pepper) and add the sugar.

Pour the cream into the soup and allow the mixture to warm through. Adjust the seasoning if necessary and ladle the soup into warmed serving bowls. Garnish each bowl with a sprinkling of the remaining garlic chives.

HOW TO ROAST A BULB OF GARLIC

Preheat the oven to 190°C/375°C/gas mark 5. Horizontally slice a bulb of garlic. Place it in kitchen foil, drizzle with a little oil, then seal tightly and bake in the oven for 45–55 minutes until the garlic has softened. Squeeze any leftover roasted garlic pulp into a sterilized jar (see page 209), add a little olive oil and store in the refrigerator.

Let this soup heat you up on a cold day. Add some crème fraîche or cream to make it extra special.

SERVES 6

5 parsnips, cut into small pieces
½ onion, chopped
Olive oil
30g (2 tbsp) butter
Salt and black pepper
1 tsp Thai green curry paste
1 tbsp chopped flat leaf parsley
400ml (1¾ cups) coconut milk
1.4 litres (6 cups) water
Crème fraîche or pouring (light) cream,
    to garnish (optional)

Curried Parsnip Soup

Place the parsnips and onion in a large saucepan over a medium heat with a drizzle of olive oil and the butter. Season with salt and black pepper. Add the curry paste and parsley, then mix the vegetables together.

Pour in the coconut milk and 850ml (3½ cups) of the water and bring the vegetables to the boil, then reduce the heat and simmer until all the vegetables are softened.

Add the remaining water gradually until you reach the desired consistency, then blitz the mixture to a smooth consistency with a handheld blender or in a food processor (in batches if necessary). Reheat the soup, then serve immediately, with a little crème fraîche or cream garnish, if desired.

This filling soup is a definite winter warmer and the crispy bacon garnish gives it good flavour. Additional garnishes would include prawns (shrimp) or shredded chicken.

SERVES 6–8

60g (4½ tbsp) butter
1 small leek, trimmed and thinly sliced
2 onions, sliced
750g (1½lb) potatoes (or 6 potatoes),
    cut into small pieces
Salt and black pepper
1.2 litres (5 cups) warm chicken stock
250ml (1 cup) pouring (light) cream
1 tbsp chopped flat leaf parsley leaves
150g (5½oz) rashers (slices) of smoked
    bacon, baked until crispy, to garnish

Potato and Bacon Soup

Melt the butter in a saucepan and add the leek and onions. Sauté gently until the onion is softened but not browned.

Add the potatoes and season with salt and black pepper, then add the stock. Bring to the boil, then reduce the heat to low and simmer for 30–40 minutes until the potatoes have softened.

Blitz the mixture to a smooth consistency using a handheld blender or in a food processor. Add the cream, then return the soup to the heat. Sprinkle with the parsley and simmer gently for a couple of minutes to reheat – do not allow the soup to boil.

To serve, divide the soup between bowls and crumble the smoked bacon on top. Serve immediately.

This wonderful combination creates a luxurious soup that is a great option for a dinner party.

SERVES 4–6

1 tbsp olive oil
1 onion, thinly sliced
2 leeks, trimmed and thinly sliced
3 garlic cloves, finely chopped
6 courgettes (zucchini), cut into chunks
500ml (2 cups) warm vegetable stock
Salt and white pepper
50g (½ cup) blanched almonds

Courgette and Almond Soup

Heat the oil in large saucepan over a medium heat. Add the onion and leeks and sauté gently for 5 minutes. Add the garlic and sauté for a further minute.

Stir the courgettes into the mixture, then reduce the heat, cover with a lid and allow the vegetables to sweat for 5 minutes.

Pour in the stock, cover the pan with a lid and bring to the boil. Lightly season with salt and white pepper, then reduce the heat and simmer for 15 minutes or until the vegetables are cooked through.

Add the blanched almonds and continue to simmer for 5 minutes to soften them. Allow the mixture to cool slightly, then blitz to a smooth consistency using a handheld blender or in a food processor (in batches if necessary). Check the seasoning and adjust as required. Reheat if necessary and serve immediately.

Watercress, which is a member of the mustard family, gives this soup its delicious peppery flavour.

2 bunches of watercress
25g (2 tbsp) butter
2 shallots, chopped
150g (5½oz) ham, diced
Salt and black pepper
2 garlic cloves, chopped
200g (7oz) potatoes (or 2 potatoes),
    cut into small pieces
100ml (½ cup) dry white wine
500ml (2 cups) warm chicken stock
½ bunch of chives, chopped
100ml (½ cup) crème fraîche

Watercress, Ham and Crème Fraîche Soup

Separate the watercress leaves from the stalks and set aside in 2 separate piles.

Heat a large saucepan and melt the butter in it. Add the shallots, ham and a pinch of salt. Cook on a medium-low heat for 2–3 minutes until the shallot is slightly caramelized and begins to take on some colour.

Add the garlic, potatoes and the watercress stalks. Season with salt and black pepper, then add the wine to deglaze the pan, scraping up the bits from the base of the pan. Continue heating until the liquid has reduce to a third.

Pour in the chicken stock, bring to the boil, then reduce the heat and simmer until the potatoes are soft.

Blitz the mixture to a smooth consistency using a handheld blender or in a food processor (in batches if necessary). Then add the watercress leaves and continue blitzing until the soup is bright green. Pass the mixture through a sieve (strainer). Now check the seasoning and adjust if necessary.

Mix the chopped chives with the crème fraîche. Reheat the soup if necessary, then serve it with a dollop of the herby crème fraîche.

You can use a combination of chicken legs and wings that are left over after Sunday lunch for this recipe, if you like. Just pluck the meat from the bones and add it to the broth.

SERVES 6

1 whole chicken, about 1.5kg (3¼lb),
    skinned and jointed into about
    8 pieces
1.4 litres (6 cups) light chicken stock
3 celery sticks, chopped
2 large carrots, halved lengthways
1 large onion, halved through the root
    end
125g (2 cups) button mushrooms, thinly
    sliced
2 bay leaves
2 tsp thyme leaves
¾ tsp black pepper
1cm (½ inch) fresh root ginger, peeled
    and chopped
2 garlic cloves, finely chopped
Salt and black pepper

Cure-all Chicken Broth

Place all the ingredients in a large saucepan. Bring to the boil, then reduce the heat and simmer for 30–40 minutes. From time to time, use a slotted spoon to skim off the scum forming on the surface.

Remove the chicken pieces from the broth and pluck the cooked meat from the bones. Add the plucked meat to the broth.

Cook for a further 5 minutes, then check the seasoning, adjusting it if necessary, and serve the broth immediately.

With a large supply of fresh fish and shellfish readily available for us at the hotel, is it any wonder that we make this delicious seafood chowder so often? I normally double the recipe and use the second batch to make a fish pie (see page 58). If you like smoked fish, you can make a delicious alternative to this recipe using smoked haddock as part of the fish mixture. Because the chowder is so quick, there is no excuse not to make it, and the added beauty of it is that it requires no accompaniment other than a large chunk of bread.

SERVES 6

12 raw Dublin Bay prawns (langoustines) or large tiger prawns (jumbo shrimp)
55g (4 tbsp) butter
1 small onion, diced
1 leek, trimmed and diced
1 small carrot, diced
1 potato, cubed
55g (2oz) smoked salmon slices, cut into strips about 5mm (¼ inch) thick

125ml (½ cup) dry white wine
425ml (1¾ cups) fish stock or water
280g (10oz) mixed fresh fish fillets (such as cod, haddock, hake and salmon), skinned and cut into bite-sized pieces
140g (5oz) mussels, scrubbed
1 tbsp chopped tarragon
200ml (1 cup) pouring (light) cream
Salt and black pepper

Arthurstown Fish Chowder

Peel the prawns, leaving the tails intact. Using a small, sharp knife, make a very shallow cut all the way down the back of the prawns and remove the black line.

Heat a large saucepan over a medium heat. Add the butter and, once it is foaming, tip in the onion, leek, carrot, potato and smoked salmon. Sauté for 2–3 minutes until softened.

Pour the wine into the pan and allow the liquid to reduce by half.

Add the fish stock or water and bring to a simmer, then add the fresh fish and shellfish.

Reduce the heat and return the pan to a simmer. Add the tarragon and cream, then season with salt and black pepper to taste. Cover with a lid and simmer gently for a further 2–3 minutes until the fish and prawns are tender and all of the mussels have opened (discard any that remain closed).

To serve, ladle the chowder into warmed serving bowls, piling plenty of the fish and shellfish into the centre of each bowl.

Always scrub mussels before you cook with them. Don't use any mussels whose shells are open before cooking, and never use any whose shells remain closed after cooking.

SERVES 6

2 tbsp olive oil
2 shallots, sliced
2 garlic cloves, crushed
1 celery stick, chopped
1 small leek, trimmed and thinly sliced
1 tsp ground turmeric
2 tbsp mild curry powder
125ml (½ cup) white wine

150ml (⅔ cup) fish stock
2kg (4½lb) mussels, scrubbed
400ml (1¾ cups) coconut milk
Salt and black pepper
Juice of ½ lemon
1 red chilli, deseeded and sliced
Flat leaf parsley or coriander (cilantro), chopped, to garnish

Curried Mussel Soup

Heat a large saucepan, add a splash of olive oil and sauté the shallots, garlic, celery and leek for about 2 minutes until softened but not browned. Next, add the turmeric and curry powder and cook for a further minute.

Pour in the white wine and reduce the liquid by half. Add the stock and bring the mixture to a simmer.

Next, add the mussels (depending on their size, you might need to add more or less stock to just cover). Put a lid on the pan and steam for about 5 minutes, until the mussels are just open.

Remove the mussels and set aside. Strain the liquid through a colander into a clean saucepan and discard the vegetables. Reduce this liquid slightly over a medium heat, then add the coconut milk and season with salt and black pepper to taste. Finish with a squeeze of lemon.

Pick half of the mussels from their shells and put them into serving bowls. Arrange the remaining mussels in their shells in the bowls (just discard any mussels that have not opened). Pour over the hot broth, scatter over some sliced chilli and chopped herbs and serve.

This hearty soup is packed full of flavours and is very filling. Try to use your favourite pale ales and cheeses, which are available at local markets.

SERVES 4–6

1 tbsp olive oil
225g (8oz) bacon lardons
    (diced bacon)
1 celery stick, finely chopped
1 onion, finely chopped
2 garlic cloves, finely chopped
1 green chilli, deseeded and sliced
1 tbsp thyme leaves

150ml (⅔ cup) pale ale or
    lager (beer)
850ml (3½ cups) chicken stock
100g (1 stick) butter
30g (3 tbsp) plain (all-purpose) flour
350ml (1½ cups) double (heavy) cream
225g (2 cups) mature (sharp) Cheddar
    cheese, grated
Salt and black pepper

Pale Ale and Cheddar Soup

Drizzle the olive oil into a large saucepan and add the bacon lardons. Cook over a moderate heat for 5–6 minutes until crisp. Remove the bacon from the pan and set aside.

Add the celery, onion, garlic, chilli and thyme leaves to the pan and cook gently until softened.

Pour half the pale ale into the saucepan and cook until the liquid has reduced by half, then add the chicken stock and simmer for 15 minutes.

In a separate small saucepan, melt the butter, add the flour and cook over a moderate heat until the flour is slightly browned, stirring continuously. Add this roux to the soup, bring back to a simmer, then cook, stirring until smooth, for a further 8 minutes.

Pour the remaining pale ale into the pan and add the cream, then stir in the cheese. Stir until the soup has thickened, then season with salt and black pepper to taste. Return the lardons to the soup and serve immediately.

Breads

Everybody has their own unique recipe for brown soda bread and this one is mine. This loaf has a firm and crusty exterior and a nice spongy centre that makes it lovely and moist. Sometimes I add in pine nuts or sesame, pumpkin, sunflower, fennel or caraway seeds for a healthy, crunchy finish. Diced dried apricots or sultanas (golden raisins) are also tasty additions. For a sweeter, darker bread, add 2 tablespoons of treacle (molasses) to the wet mix.

MAKES A 900G (9-INCH) LOAF

350g (2¾ cups) wholemeal (whole-wheat) flour
55g (⅓ cup) plain (all-purpose) flour
2 tsp bicarbonate of (baking) soda, sifted
Pinch of salt
55g (⅔ cup) porridge (rolled) oats
2 large (US extra-large) eggs

2 tsp sunflower oil, plus extra for greasing
500ml (2 cups) buttermilk (or use natural/plain yogurt or fresh milk mixed with the juice of 1 lemon)
Handful of seeds or extra porridge oats, for sprinkling

Traditional Brown Soda Bread

Preheat the oven to 160°C/325°F/gas mark 3. Lightly grease a 900g (9 x 5 x 3-inch) loaf tin.

Put the flours, bicarbonate of soda, salt and porridge oats into a large mixing bowl and mix them well.

In a separate bowl, beat the eggs together with the oil. Add this to the dry mixture.

Next, mix in the buttermilk. The mixture should have a sloppy consistency. Pour into the prepared loaf tin and smooth the top with a wet spoon. Sprinkle some seeds or porridge oats across the top, then bake for 1 hour. After the hour has elapsed, remove the bread from the tin and return it to the oven to bake for a further 20 minutes. (Alternatively, if you would prefer bread rolls, spoon the mixture into a greased 12-cup muffin tin and bake at 180°C/350°F/gas mark 4 for 25–30 minutes.)

Remove the bread from the oven and allow it to cool on a wire rack before serving. This loaf will keep fresh for 4–5 days and is suitable for freezing.

Soda bread is one of Ireland's specialities and is still baked in many country kitchens. This variation on the traditional recipe requires the oatmeal to be soaked in buttermilk overnight prior to cooking.

MAKES A 900G (9-INCH) LOAF

280g (3 cups) fine oatmeal (oat bran)
600ml (2½ cups) buttermilk
Oil, for greasing
450g (3⅔ cups) plain (all-purpose) flour
Pinch of salt
2 tsp bicarbonate of (baking) soda

Oatmeal Soda Bread

In a large bowl, steep the oatmeal in the buttermilk overnight.

The next day, preheat the oven to 180°C/350°F/gas mark 4. Lightly grease a 900g (9 x 5 x 3-inch) loaf tin.

Sift the flour, salt and bicarbonate of soda into the soaked oatmeal, then stir to combine until the mixture has a soft consistency, but is not sloppy. It may be necessary to add a little extra buttermilk, but you don't want the dough to be too wet. Turn it onto a lightly floured work surface, pat the dough into shape, then place it in the prepared loaf tin. Bake for 50–60 minutes.

Remove the bread from the oven, let it cool a little in the tin, then turn it onto a wire rack to cool down before serving. This loaf will keep fresh for 4–5 days and is suitable for freezing.

Plain scones, served with raspberry jam and freshly whipped double (heavy) cream, are my absolute favourite. This reliable recipe will give you perfect scones every time. To make fruit scones, soak 70g (½ cup) sultanas (golden raisins) in a little orange juice or whiskey for 30 minutes and throw these into the mixture just before you add the egg and milk. Another alternative is to replace 25g (3 tbsp) of the flour with ground almonds, which gives a nice rich flavour to the scones. You could also add 70g (2½oz) grated white or dark chocolate, or the grated rind of an orange.

MAKES 10 SCONES

400g (3¼ cups) plain (all-purpose) flour
1 tsp baking powder
115g (⅔ cup) caster (superfine) sugar
Pinch of salt
175g (1½ sticks) cold butter, cubed
1 egg

125ml (½ cup) buttermilk
Egg wash, made with 1 egg yolk beaten with 1 tsp milk
Granulated sugar, for sprinkling
Icing (confectioners') sugar, for dusting

Buttermilk Scones

Preheat the oven to 160°C/325°F/gas mark 3. Line a baking sheet with greaseproof (wax) paper or nonstick baking paper.

Sift the flour, baking powder, caster sugar and salt into a large bowl, then rub in the butter with your fingertips.

In a small bowl, beat the egg, then add this to the dry ingredients. Now add the buttermilk little by little and mix together until you have a soft, pliable dough. If the mixture is too wet and loose at this stage, add in a little extra flour.

Transfer the mixture to a floured work surface and flatten it out to about 2cm (¾ inch) in depth. Using a 5cm (2-inch) diameter scone or cookie cutter, or the similar-sized open end of a drinking glass, cut out 10 circles and transfer them to the prepared baking sheet. (You can freeze the uncooked shaped scones in freezer bags at this stage, if you like, then cook them from frozen at a later date.)

Brush the top of each scone with egg wash and sprinkle with a little granulated sugar. Bake for 20 minutes. (If you are baking frozen uncooked scones, simply brush the tops with egg wash, sprinkle with sugar and bake in an oven preheated to 140°C/275°F/gas mark 1 for 30–40 minutes.)

Remove the scones from the oven and transfer them to a wire rack. Dust with icing sugar. Serve the scones either warm or cold.

Although the traditional bread-making method below can take a while, it's definitely worth the wait because it produces, without a doubt, the best-tasting bread. The first step is to make a starter dough and feed it every day with flour and water. It's very important to use natural spring water or distilled water because chlorinated water will not work so well.

MAKES 2 X 500G (8½-INCH) LOAVES

500g (3⅔ cups) strong white bread
  flour, plus extra for dusting
200ml (1 cup) warm water
20g (3¼ tsp) salt
1 tbsp caster (superfine) sugar

FOR THE SOURDOUGH STARTER
200g (1½ cups) strong white bread flour
200ml (1 cup) distilled water (or use
  tap water that has been allowed to
  stand in a glass for 24 hours)

Sourdough Bread

First make the sourdough starter. Place half the flour with half the water in a plastic or glass container and stir with a wooden spoon until combined. Seal the container loosely with clingfilm (plastic wrap) or a clean towel to allow the dough to breathe and set aside at room temperature. 'Feed' the starter every day for 5 days with 20ml (4 tsp) of the remaining water and 20g (2½ tbsp) of the remaining flour, mixing a little with a wooden spoon. The result should be light and aerated because the process traps natural airborne yeast particles in the flour-and-water mix, creating a living yeast colony. The sourdough mixture is ready 24 hours after the fifth and final feed, at which point you can continue with the bread recipe.

Put the flour into a bowl and add 300ml (1¼ cups) of your sourdough starter. Then add the warm water, salt and sugar. Mix it all altogether, then turn the mixture onto a lightly floured work surface and knead for 10–15 minutes, or until it starts to come away from the surface. If you prefer, you can use a bread machine or an electric mixer with a bread hook attachment to knead the bread.

Once the dough is stretchy, put it into a bowl and leave it somewhere warm for 2 hours to rise.

Turn the dough onto a lightly floured surface and push your knuckles into the dough to knock out air from it. Divide into 2 equal pieces.

Dust 2 proving baskets or 500g (8½-inch) loaf tins with flour. Roll each piece of dough in flour to stop them from sticking. Put them into the baskets or tins, cover with a clean tea (dish) towel and leave in a warm place, this time for 4–8 hours, to rise again.

To bake the loaves without loaf tins, heat the oven to 240°C/475°F/gas mark 9 and heat a baking stone or a heavy metal baking sheet until very hot. Carefully turn the risen dough onto the hot sheet or stone – be careful not to knock any air out of them. Give each piece of dough a cut along the top, then place in the oven with a small ovenproof container of hot water to create steam and allow an even crust to form. If you are baking the loaves in tins, simply place them in the oven. Bake for 30 minutes until golden.

Remove the bread from the oven, dust with flour and allow the loaves to cool down on a wire rack before serving. These loaves will keep fresh for 2–3 days.

This lovely crusty bread makes fabulous bruschetta and is perfect for a 'doorstep' sandwich. Substitute spelt flour for the rye flour, if you prefer.

MAKES 4 SMALL LOAVES

40g (1½oz) fresh yeast
1 litre (4¼ cups) lukewarm water
1.5kg (11 cups) strong white bread flour,
    plus extra for dusting
400g (4 cups) rye flour
35g (2 tbsp) salt

Corkscrew Bread

Dust a large baking sheet with flour and set aside. In a large bowl, dissolve the yeast in the lukewarm water, then add the flours and salt and mix well for 5–7 minutes to allow the mixture to come together into a dough.

Cover the bowl with clingfilm (plastic wrap) and leave the dough at room temperature (best would be 24°C/75°F) for 45 minutes to rise.

Cut the dough lengthways into 4 and roll each piece into a 40cm (16 inch) length. Sprinkle a little bit of flour over the top of each piece, then twist the ends to create corkscrews.

Place each corkscrew onto the prepared baking sheet and leave for 30 minutes to rise again. Meanwhile, preheat the oven to 230°C/450°F/gas mark 8.

Sprinkle a light stream of water onto the bread with your fingers (this helps to form a crust) and dust with flour. Bake for 10 minutes, then decrease the temperature to 200°C/350°F/gas mark 6 and bake for a further 10–15 minutes or until each loaf sounds hollow when the bottom is tapped.

Remove the bread from the oven and allow the loaves to cool on a wire rack before serving. They will keep fresh for 1–2 days.

FRESH YEAST OR DRIED YEAST?

Fresh yeast is generally available in bakeries or supermarkets that have their own in-house bakery. I like to use fresh yeast, but you can replace the fresh yeast with the same amount of easy blend dried (active dry) yeast if you prefer. The only difference between fresh and dried yeast is that you add dried yeast straight to the flour, while fresh yeast should be dissolved in warm water first.

Waterford Blaa is a doughy white bread roll that is a speciality particular to both the city and county of Waterford. The blaa is very soft and is covered in white flour.

MAKES 6–10 ROLLS

500g (3⅔ cups) strong white bread
    flour, plus extra for dusting
10g (1½ tsp) salt
10g (½ tbsp) butter, plus extra for
    greasing
20g (¾oz) fresh yeast
1 tsp caster (superfine) sugar
275ml (1 cup + 2 tbsp) lukewarm water

Waterford Blaa

Place the flour and salt in a large mixing bowl, add the butter and mix together.

In a bowl, dissolve the yeast and sugar in the lukewarm water and leave for 10 minutes in a warm place to activate.

Pour the mixture into the butter and flour and mix until combined. Knead the dough for about 5 minutes until it becomes smooth and elastic. Then cover the bowl with clingfilm (plastic wrap) or a damp cloth and leave in a warm place for 45 minutes to rise.

Now knock back the dough. To do this, push your knuckles into the dough to knock out air from it. Cover the bowl and leave the dough to rise for a further 15 minutes. The short rest time gives the gluten time to relax, making shaping easier.

Divide the dough into 6–10 similar-sized pieces. Roll each piece into a smooth ball and arrange them on a greased baking sheet, spaced 3–4cm (1¼–1½ inches) apart to allow them to link together during the final rising. Dredge with a little extra flour and leave them for 50 minutes to rise.

Preheat the oven to 220°C/425°F/gas mark 7.

Place the bread in the oven with a small ovenproof container of hot water to create steam and allow an even crust to form. Bake for 15–20 minutes until the rolls sound hollow when their bottoms are tapped.

Cool on a wire rack before serving. Blaas quickly lose their freshness and are best consumed within a few hours of making.

The aroma of this freshly baked bread topped with sweet caramelized onion will have you coming back for more. I normally make this recipe into rolls and use them for burgers (see page 100) or sandwiches. However, it can also be cooked in a large loaf.

MAKES 1 LOAF OR 12 ROLLS

30g (1oz) fresh yeast
400ml (1¾ cups) lukewarm water
650g (5¼ cups) plain (all-purpose)
    flour
20g (3¼ tsp) salt
Egg wash, made with 1 egg yolk beaten
    with 1 tsp of milk
115g (⅓ cup) Red Onion Marmalade
    (see page 215)

Caramelized Onion Bread

Place the yeast and water in a medium-sized bowl and stir with a fork to dissolve the yeast. Allow the mixture to stand for about 3 minutes.

Place the flour and salt in another bowl and add the yeast mixture. Mix with your fingers for 2–3 minutes to incorporate the flour, scraping the sides of the bowl and folding the dough over itself, until the mixture gathers into a rough mass.

Move the dough to a lightly floured work surface and knead for 6–8 minutes until it becomes supple and somewhat elastic. The dough will be very sticky at first; keep your hands and the work surface lightly floured and use a dough scraper, if necessary, to prevent it from sticking and building up on the work surface. As you continue kneading, the dough will become more elastic and easier to handle.

Shape the dough into a loose ball, return it to the bowl and cover it with clingfilm (plastic wrap). Leave it in a warm place for about 50 minutes to rise.

Knead the dough again on the lightly floured surface for 2–3 minutes or until it becomes very smooth and springy. Shape the dough into a round loaf or divide it into 12 pieces and roll each piece into a round shape. Place on a greased baking sheet, brush with egg wash and spoon the onion marmalade on top. Leave the dough to rise at room temperature for about 1 hour or until it looks slightly puffy.

Preheat the oven to 180°C/350°F/gas mark 4.

Bake the loaf for about 20 minutes or the rolls for 15 minutes, until deep golden brown and the bottom sounds hollow when tapped.

Remove the bread from the oven and allow to cool on a wire rack before serving. It will keep fresh for a day.

One of the nicest breakfasts or mid-morning snacks is this bread, made into traditional triangular 'farls', and served with some fried eggs. (Drizzle a little oil into the pan and crack in the eggs. Cook for 2 minutes, then turn and cook for 30 seconds. Serve on a slice of potato bread with a sprinkling of parsley.) It is best to use mashed potato that is still warm for this potato bread recipe. Alternatively, if using cold leftover mash, pop it into the oven to warm up before mixing with the other ingredients.

MAKES 6 FARLS

280g (1⅓ cups) warm mashed potato
½ tsp salt
½ tsp black pepper
55g (4 tbsp) butter
85g (⅔ cup) plain (all-purpose) flour,
    plus extra for dusting

Potato Bread

Place the mashed potato into a large bowl and season with the salt and black pepper.

Melt the butter and add this to the potato, then sift in the flour and mix well to make a pliable dough.

Lightly dust your work surface with a little flour, then turn the potato dough onto it and roll into a circle that is roughly 1cm (½ inch) thick and 25cm (9½ inches) in diameter. Now divide it into 6 triangles (farls).

Meanwhile, heat a large, heavy-based nonstick frying pan or griddle (ridged grill) over a moderate heat. (Traditionally, no fat or oil would be added to the pan to cook potato bread.) Cook the farls for 3–4 minutes on each side. Serve immediately.

Fish and Seafood

This dish is a classic that is as rich and luxurious as it sounds – perfect for a special occasion.

SERVES 2

2 lobsters, about 750g (1½lb) each
250g (1¼ cups) mashed potato
50g (4 tbsp) butter
Juice of ½ lemon

FOR THE MUSTARD CREAM SAUCE
40g (3 tbsp) butter, cubed
1 tsp Dalkey mustard (or use
    wholegrain mustard)
4 tbsp white wine
100ml (½ cup) double (heavy) cream
1 tbsp chopped chives
Salt and black pepper

Oven-baked Lobster with Dalkey Mustard Cream Sauce

Preheat the oven to 240°C/475°F/gas mark 9.

Cook the lobsters in boiling salted water for 2–3 minutes, then plunge into cold water to stop the cooking process. Place on a chopping board and cut in half lengthways along the back. Remove and discard the head meat and pink coral. Pipe or spoon some mashed potato into the head cavity. Crack the lobster claws with a heavy knife or cleaver, then lay the lobsters shell-side down in a roasting dish.

Melt half the butter in a small saucepan over a moderate heat and add the lemon juice. Pour over the lobster tail and potato. Place in the oven and bake for 12 minutes.

Meanwhile, make the sauce. Melt half the butter in a small frying pan, add the mustard and stir to combine. Pour in the white wine, bring to the boil and then allow the sauce to reduce by half. Pour in the cream, stir to combine and cook until the sauce further reduces and coats the back of a spoon. Remove from the heat, add the chives and season with salt and pepper to taste. Add the remaining butter and swirl through the sauce until it gets a lovely glossy finish. If the sauce splits, add a little more cream to rescue it.

Remove the lobster from the oven, drizzle the cream over the top of the meat and serve immediately.

This is my own take on fish *en papillote* (in a paper parcel).
It can be cooked in a barbecue pit on the beach or baked in the
oven. If the salmon is too large, simply cut it into portions and
wrap these individually.

SERVES 8–10

1 whole salmon, about 3–4kg
   (6½–8¾lb), cleaned and gutted, and
   head and tail removed if you wish
Bunch of fresh herbs (use dill, flat leaf
   parsely or oregano)
1 lemon, sliced
Salt and black pepper (omit the salt
   if cooking in the pit – see below)
100g (1 stick) butter, sliced

Whole Salmon Baked in a Smouldering Pit

Wash the fish thoroughly and pat it dry with some kitchen paper (paper towels).
Place the herbs, lemon slices and seasoning into the cavity of the salmon and add
the butter slices outside along the top. Lay the salmon on a large sheet of nonstick
baking paper and fold to enclose.

To bake in a barbecue pit, you will first need to dig a hole about 30cm (12 inches)
longer than the salmon and about 40–60cm (16–24 inches) deep. Secure the
sides of the pit with a few large stones around the edge. Heat the pit like a normal
charcoal barbecue until a layer of white ashes has formed on top of the charcoal, but
allow longer than normal for the coals to reach the correct temperature. Wrap the
salmon tightly in 10 sheets of newspaper and immerse the package into a bucket of
seawater. When the paper has absorbed the water, lay the parcel in the pit, cover
with some embers and cook for about 1¼ hours. To test if the salmon is cooked, tear
the parcel slightly near the centre of the fish, pull back the skin and pierce the flesh
– the juices should run clear and the flesh should be slightly opaque.

Alternatively, preheat the oven to 180°C/350°F/gas mark 4. Wrap the salmon
tightly in 10 sheets of damp newspaper and tie up the parcel or package with some
kitchen string, ensuring that the edges of the paper are tucked in. Place the parcel
onto a large baking sheet and pop it into the oven for about 50 minutes until the
salmon is cooked through (see above for testing that it is ready).

Serve with Beetroot and Baby Potato Salad (see page 140) and Hollandaise Sauce
(see page 205).

When the mackerel are in at Slade, it's standing-room only on the pier as hundreds of people descend to catch the freshest fish for supper. As mackerel is an oily fish, I would recommend soaking the fillets in some salty water for about 20 minutes before smoking because this will help to dry out the flesh and improve the flavour of the dish. If you do not have a smoker, you can use a wok instead.

SERVES 4

8 mackerel fillets, about 90g (3½oz) each
1 tbsp olive oil
Salt and black pepper
200g (7oz) rocket (arugula) leaves
Juice of ½ lemon
Lemon wedges, to serve

FOR THE BLACKCURRANT SAUCE
200g (1¾ cups) blackcurrants
4 tbsp sugar
4 tbsp sherry vinegar

Smoked Slade Mackerel Fillets with Blackcurrant Sauce

First make the blackcurrant sauce. Place the blackcurrants and sugar in a saucepan over a moderate heat and cook for 2–3 minutes until the juices are bursting from the fruit. Add the vinegar, then remove the pan from the heat and set aside.

If you have a smoker, soak some wood chips in water, then place them in the bottom of the smoker. Sit it on the hob or stove to heat, or put some burning charcoal on the chips until hot. Place a piece of kitchen foil on the smoker rack and pierce some vents in it with a sharp knife.

Alternatively, place some soaked wood chips in the bottom of a wok, cover them with kitchen foil and pierce some vents in the foil with a sharp knife. Position a wire rack on which to cook the fish inside the wok, cover with a lid and heat the wok over a low to medium heat until smoke builds up under the lid.

Brush the mackerel fillets on each side with olive oil, then season with salt and black pepper and lay the fish on the foil. Cook in the smoker, as per the manufacturer's instructions, for about 15 minutes or cook in the wok for about 10 minutes.

Remove the fish from the smoker. Place 2 fillets overlapping on each plate and serve with some rocket leaves drizzled in lemon juice and seasoned with salt and black pepper, with a spoonful of blackcurrant sauce and a lemon wedge.

Lemon sole is a particularly delicate fish, both in texture and flavour. Of the various species of sole, this one is the most widely available and, all in all, offers good value for money.

SERVES 4

500g (1lb 2oz) baby new potatoes
Salt and black pepper
1 tbsp olive oil
2 lemon or black sole, about 250–300g
   (9–10½oz) each, cleaned, gutted and
   fin removed
100g (1 stick) butter
Juice of 1 lemon
2 tbsp capers, rinsed
2 tbsp finely chopped flat leaf parsley
1 lemon, sliced, to garnish

Sole with Capers and Lemon Sauce

Place the potatoes in a large saucepan of water with a pinch of salt. Bring to the boil, then reduce the heat and simmer for 20 minutes. Drain the potatoes, then return them to the pan and cover with a cloth to keep warm. When you are ready to serve, cut the potatoes into slices 2cm (¾ inch) thick.

In the meantime, cook the sole. Heat the oil in a large nonstick frying pan over a moderate heat, place the sole into the pan and cook over a low heat for 2–3 minutes on each side until the fish is just barely cooked through and is slightly browned around the edges. It is important not to shake the pan because this may cause the fish to break.

Add the butter and heat until it is frothy and has a hazelnut colour. Add a squeeze of lemon juice, the capers and parsley and cook for a further 30 seconds, then transfer the fish onto serving plates.

Put the warmed sliced potato into the empty pan and toss in the juices, then transfer to the serving plates.

Taste the pan juices to check the seasoning, then pour the sauce over the fish. Serve immediately, garnished with lemon slices.

The butter takes on a beautiful brown colour with a nutty flavour that complements this delicious fish so well.

SERVES 4

50g (⅓ cup) plain (all-purpose) flour
Salt and black pepper
4 skate wings, about 225g (8oz) each
100g (1 stick) butter
Juice of 1½ lemons
2 tbsp capers, rinsed
Finely chopped flat leaf parsley

Skate with Beurre Noisette

Season the flour with some salt and black pepper, then spread it out on a plate. One by one, lay the skate wings on the flour and lightly coat both sides. Pat them gently to remove any excess flour.

Melt 50g (4 tbsp) of the butter in a large nonstick frying pan. Add the skate wings, 2 at a time, and fry over a medium heat for about 5 minutes on each side. The flesh should be firm and white and the skin should be golden. Transfer the fish to a warmed plate, cover and keep warm.

Return the pan to the heat, then add the remaining butter (do not have the heat too high or the butter will burn). Once the butter has melted and turned golden brown, remove the pan from the heat and add the lemon juice and capers. Taste the sauce to decide if any further seasoning is required. Add some finely chopped parsley to it, then pour it over the skate and serve immediately.

Trout are a fantastic source of minerals, including selenium and iron, and they are also rich in omega-3 fats. Wrapping the trout in some streaky bacon makes this dish so delicious. The flaked almonds add texture and flavour to the dish, but can be omitted if preferred.

SERVES 4

3 tbsp plain (all-purpose) flour
4 trout fillets, about 225g (8oz) each,
    cleaned, gutted and skinned
12 rashers (slices) of smoked streaky
    (fatty) bacon
Salt and black pepper
2 tbsp oil
150g (1¼ sticks) butter
4 tbsp flaked (slivered) almonds
    (optional)
2 tbsp roughly chopped tarragon
Juice of 1 lemon

Trout Fillets with Streaky Bacon and Flaked Almonds

Lightly flour the trout, wrap each fillet in 3 slices of streaky bacon, then season with salt and black pepper.

Drizzle the oil into a frying pan on a moderate to high heat. Place the wrapped trout in the pan and caramelize the bacon for 2 minutes on each side. Reduce the heat, add 100g (1 stick) of the butter and leave the trout to cook on a low heat with the butter foaming for about 5 minutes on each side.

Transfer the fish to a warmed plate, and pat dry to remove the excess butter.

Add the remaining butter to the pan and allow it to foam, then add the almonds, if using, and fry lightly. Sprinkle with the tarragon, then add the lemon juice to deglaze the pan, scraping up any bits from the base of the pan. Spoon the flavoured almonds over the trout and serve immediately.

While pike is notoriously bony, it's worth the effort of pin-boning because the flesh is deliciously rich and meaty.

SERVES 4

50g (⅓ cup) plain (all-purpose) flour
Salt and black pepper
3 tbsp green peppercorns in brine
4 pike fillets, about 160–180g
   (5½–6½oz) each (ling or perch may
   be used instead)
1 tbsp rapeseed (canola) oil
50g (2 tbsp) butter
1 shallot, chopped
4 tbsp white wine vinegar
100ml (½ cup) water

Pike with Vinegar and Crushed Peppercorns

In a small bowl, season the flour with some salt and black pepper.

Sprinkle the peppercorns over both sides of the fillets followed by the seasoned flour.

Heat the oil and butter in a large nonstick frying pan. Add the fish and fry over a moderate heat for 4–6 minutes on each side. Transfer the fillets to a warmed plate, cover and keep warm.

Add the shallot to the pan and gently heat until softened. Pour in the vinegar and reduce completely, then add in the water and reduce by three-quarters.

Season to taste, drizzle the reduction over the fish and serve with steamed potatoes.

The simplest way is sometimes the best way, and a little butter is all you need to enhance the delicate flavour of this tasty fish.

SERVES 4

2 tbsp rapeseed (canola) oil
4 halibut fillets, about 150g
    (5½oz) each
Sea salt and black pepper
20g (1½ tbsp) butter
300g (10oz) samphire (sea asparagus),
    to serve

Pan-fried Halibut with Samphire

Heat a little oil in a large nonstick frying pan over a moderate heat, then lay the fish in the pan, flesh-side down. Season with a little sea salt and black pepper, then reduce the heat and cook for 3–4 minutes until the flesh is just opaque and slightly coloured.

Using a fish slice, gently turn the fish over, season again, if liked, then add the butter to the pan and allow it to melt. Spoon the foaming butter over the fish and cook for a further 2–3 minutes (depending on its thickness). Transfer to a warmed plate, cover and keep warm.

Add the samphire to the pan and toss in the fish juices and butter. Cook for 2–3 minutes, then divide between 4 serving plates. Place a fillet of fish on each bed of samphire. Serve with Crushed Baby Potatoes (see page 166).

This wonderfully fragrant dish is very easy to prepare, as is the parcel of vegetables accompanying it. Make it with the fish heads removed, if you feel they won't endear themselves to your guests.

SERVES 4

4 whole sea bass, about 500g (1lb 2oz) each (not overly large), cleaned and gutted
1 lemon, sliced
12 sprigs of tarragon
12 sprigs of coriander (cilantro)
3kg (13½ cups) rock (kosher) salt
4 egg whites
Grated rind of 2 lemons
Olive oil, for drizzling

FOR THE VEGETABLE PAPILLOTE
2 (bell) peppers (use a mix of red and green), deseeded and thinly sliced
2 red onions, thinly sliced
5mm (¼ inch) fresh root ginger, peeled and thinly sliced
2 carrots, thinly sliced
2 ripe tomatoes, thinly sliced
1 lime, thinly sliced
Salt and black pepper
300ml (1¼ cups) white wine
100ml (½ cup) fish stock

Whole Roasted Sea Bass in a Sea Salt Crust

Preheat the oven to 190°C/375°F/gas mark 5.

Place the sea bass in a dish and insert the lemon slices, tarragon and coriander sprigs into the cavities.

In a bowl, mix the rock salt, egg whites and lemon rind to make a paste.

Set a baking sheet on your work surface and spread with a layer of the salt paste. Lay the sea bass on the salt, drizzle a little oil over the fish and cover with the remaining salt. Transfer the baking sheet to the oven and bake the fish for 20–25 minutes (depending on its size).

For the papillote, mix the thinly sliced ingredients in a bowl with some seasoning. Place them in the middle of a large square of nonstick baking paper in a roasting pan, drizzle with the wine and stock and fold the paper around them to form a parcel. Bake with the sea bass for 15 minutes.

These prawns have a lovely kick that will entice anyone. Because they are not cooked, it's important that they are eaten on the day of preparation and that all the ingredients are as fresh as possible.

SERVES 4

1 red or green chilli, deseeded and very
    finely chopped
1 tsp cayenne pepper
1 tsp ground paprika
1 tsp ground cumin
½ tsp mustard powder
1 tsp salt
1 tbsp olive oil, plus extra for drizzling
Juice of 2 limes
16 large raw Dublin Bay prawns
    (langoustines), peeled and deveined
    (see page 22)
250g (1⅔ cups) vine cherry tomatoes,
    halved
8 slices of crusty bread
1 tbsp finely chopped flat leaf parsley,
    to garnish

Devilled Dublin Bay Prawns

In a bowl, mix together the chilli, spices, mustard and salt. Drizzle in the olive oil and lime juice to make a loose paste. Add the prawns, cover and leave to marinate in the refrigerator for a few hours.

When you are ready to serve, place a layer of tomatoes on the crusty bread and drizzle with some olive oil. Place 2 prawns on each slice of bread, allowing 2 slices/4 prawns per person. Sprinkle over some finely chopped parsley and serve immediately.

This is a stew-like dish, packed full of the flavours of the sea. Be careful not to overcook the clams so they retain their succulence and juiciness. Add some pieces of chorizo to the stew for further depth of flavour, if desired.

SERVES 6

1 tbsp olive oil
30g (2 tbsp) butter
2 large onions, sliced into thin rings
1 garlic clove, chopped
3 tbsp balsamic vinegar
300ml (1¼ cups) fish or chicken stock
2 x 400g (14½oz) cans chopped
    tomatoes
1 tbsp chopped flat leaf parsley, plus
    1 tbsp extra for sprinkling
1 tbsp chopped coriander (cilantro)
Salt and black pepper
900g (2lb) fresh cod, cubed
450g (1lb) clams, in the shell, scrubbed

Ragout of Clams and Cod

Heat the oil and butter in a large saucepan, then add the onions and garlic and sauté gently until the onion has softened but not caramelized.

Stir in the balsamic vinegar, then add the stock and cook until it has reduced by two-thirds.

Next, add the tomatoes and herbs and cook for a further 10 minutes. Season with salt and black pepper to taste.

Now add the cod to the sauce, then the clams. Cover and cook for 5–8 minutes until the cod is cooked and the clams have opened (discard any that remain closed). Sprinkle with the remaining parsley and serve immediately with some crusty bread or basmati or other long-grain rice.

Fish was traditionally eaten on Fridays in homes throughout Ireland, served with a topping of creamy mashed potato – what could be more comforting? Try to get hold of naturally smoked fish instead of dyed fish.

SERVES 4–6

300ml (1¼ cups) milk
250g (9oz) smoked cod
250g (9oz) smoked haddock
60g (4½ tbsp) butter
1 onion, finely diced
150g (2 cups) button mushrooms,
    sliced
3 tbsp plain (all-purpose) flour
1 tsp mustard
1 tbsp chopped flat leaf parsley
1 tbsp lemon juice
Salt and black pepper

900g (2lb) potatoes (or 8 potatoes),
    cut into chunks
100ml (½ cup) pouring (light) cream
30g (2 tbsp) butter
60g (½ cup) Cheddar cheese, grated

Duncannon Smoked Fish Pie

Preheat the oven to 180°C/350°F/gas mark 4.

Place the milk in a saucepan and add the fish. Bring to a simmer and poach the fish over a moderate heat for 6–8 minutes until it is softened. Remove the fish with a slotted spoon and flake it onto a plate, ensuring all the bones are removed. Keep the flaked fish warm. Strain the milk liquid into a jug or small bowl and set aside.

In a separate saucepan, melt the butter, then add the onion and mushrooms and cook until softened. Remove the pan from the heat and sprinkle in the flour. Gradually add the milk liquid, stirring continuously until the sauce is thickened. Add the mustard, parsley and lemon juice, season with some salt and black pepper and stir to combine. Add the flaked fish to the sauce, then pile the whole lot into an ovenproof dish.

In the meantime, place the potatoes in a saucepan of salted water, bring to the boil and cook for 20–25 minutes until softened. Drain well, add the cream and butter and mash to ensure all lumps are removed. Season with some salt and black pepper.

Spoon the potato mixture over the fish and top with the cheese. Pop into the oven for 20–25 minutes until piping hot. Serve immediately.

This dish of plump and juicy mussels in a fragrant broth requires only some crusty bread to mop up the juices. It is ever such a quick supper to make and quite economical, too!

SERVES 4–6

1.5kg (3lb) mussels, scrubbed
225ml (1 cup) white wine
55g (4 tbsp) butter
2 shallots, chopped
2 garlic cloves, finely chopped
8 rashers (slices) of streaky (fatty)
   bacon, chopped
2 large tomatoes, deseeded
   and chopped
1 tbsp plain (all-purpose) flour
2 tbsp chopped flat leaf parsley

Kilmore Quay Mussels with Bacon and White Wine

Clean the mussels and discard any that don't close when sharply tapped.

Place the mussels in a large saucepan and cover with the wine. Cook for 3–4 minutes, shaking the pan once or twice, until the mussels are open. Transfer them to a bowl and discard any that do not open. Strain the cooking liquid into a separate bowl to remove any grit or impurities and set this and the mussels aside.

Melt half the butter in a pan over a low heat and add the shallots and garlic. Add the bacon, increase the heat to medium and cook for a few minutes until the bacon is crisp. Now add the tomatoes and cook until softened.

Mash the flour and the remaining butter in a bowl, then add this mixture to the pan, piece by piece. At the same time, slowly add the mussel cooking liquid. If you find that the sauce is too thick, add a little water to loosen the mixture.

Reheat the mussels in the sauce, then sprinkle with the parsley. Serve immediately with some crusty bread.

The delicate flavour of the scallops and the crisp pastry are a lovely combination. Although fresh scallops can be expensive, it's a case of a little goes a long way in this recipe. Drizzle the tartlets with some Wild Garlic Pesto (see page 208) to add extra flavour, if you like.

SERVES 4

2 x sheets of puff pastry, each about
   30 x 20cm (12 x 8 inches)
Egg wash, made with 1 egg, beaten with
   1 tsp milk
8 fresh scallops
4 tbsp extra virgin olive oil, plus extra
   for greasing
1 tsp finely shredded tarragon leaves
1 tbsp sea salt
1 tbsp ground black pepper

TO SERVE
200g (7oz) lamb's lettuce (mâche) or
   baby leaves or greens
Juice of 1 lemon
Lemon wedges

Dunmore East Fresh Scallop Tartlets

Preheat the oven to 190°C/375°F/gas mark 5. Grease a baking sheet.

Roll out the puff pastry and, using a 10cm (4-inch) diameter biscuit (cookie) cutter, cut out four large circles. Place them on the prepared sheet and brush with the egg wash.

Slice the scallops into discs that are about 1cm (½ inch) thick. Place them on the pastry circles so that they are slightly overlapping, drizzle with a little of the olive oil, sprinkle with tarragon and season with salt and black pepper.

Bake for 12–15 minutes or until the pastry is golden brown and the scallops are just cooked. Remove from the oven, drizzle with some more olive oil and serve immediately with lemon-dressed lamb's lettuce and lemon wedges.

These small gateaux are perfect for a dinner party because they can be prepared several hours in advance, ready to be brought back to room temperature and dressed with a little salad.

SERVES 4

225g (8oz) smoked salmon
225g (1 cup) cream cheese
1 tbsp chopped chives
Juice of ½ lemon

FOR THE PANCAKES
115g (1 cup) plain (all-purpose) flour
Salt and black pepper

1 small (US medium) egg
About 150ml (⅔ cup) milk
Sunflower oil, for frying

TO SERVE
25g (1oz) baby salad leaves or greens
2–3 tbsp Dalkey Mustard Dressing
   (see page 207)
Lemon wedges, to serve
Chives, to garnish

Smoked Salmon Gateaux

First make the pancakes. Sift the flour into a bowl with a pinch of salt, then make a well in the centre. Break the egg into the well and add a little of the milk. Mix the liquid ingredients together, then gradually beat in the surrounding flour until the mixture is smooth. Beat in enough of the remaining milk for the mixture to achieve the consistency of thin cream. Cover with clingfilm (plastic wrap) and leave to stand in the refrigerator for 20 minutes.

Heat a heavy-based frying pan. When hot, brush with the minimum of oil. Pour in a small amount of the batter – about a quarter of the mix is right. Swirl it around until it is evenly and thinly spread across the pan. Cook over a moderate to high heat for about 1 minute or until the edges are curling and the underside is golden. Flip over and cook the other side for 30 seconds or so until golden. Transfer the pancake to a plate and repeat this step until you have 4 pancakes, lightly oiling the pan between cooking each one. Leave to cool.

Using a 5cm (2-inch) cutter that is 5cm (2 inches) deep, stamp out 3 discs from each pancake so you have 12 in total. Stamp out 8 discs from the smoked salmon using the same cutter.

Whip the cream cheese in a bowl with the chives and lemon juice. Season to taste.

To assemble the gateaux, line the same cutter with clingfilm (plastic wrap) and set it on a flat surface. Put a pancake disc into the bottom of the cutter, spread a spoonful of the cream cheese over it, cover with a smoked salmon disc and add another layer of cream cheese. Repeat these layers and finish with a pancake disc. Carefully remove the cutter, leaving the clingfilm in place. Repeat until you have 4 stacks in total. Unwrap each stack and place on individual serving plates.

Place the salad leaves in a bowl, season and add enough of the dressing to lightly coat the leaves. Add a pile to each plate. Drizzle around the remaining dressing and garnish with the lemon wedges and extra chives.

TWOMEY'S
SNUG-BAR
For a
QUIET

WEXFORD

Poultry and Game

These sticky, hot and spicy chicken thighs will make your mouth sizzle!

SERVES 4

4 boneless chicken thighs, about
    100–120g (3½–4¼oz) each
100ml (½ cup) teriyaki sauce
3 tbsp rapeseed (canola) oil
400ml (1¾ cups) warm chicken stock
1 tbsp rice vinegar
30g (2 tbsp) butter

FOR THE STUFFING

70g (1½ cups) fresh breadcrumbs
2 egg yolks
3 tbsp Parmesan cheese, finely
    grated
4 tsp olive oil
2 tbsp chopped fresh coriander (cilantro)
4 garlic cloves, chopped
1cm (½ inch) fresh root ginger, peeled
    and grated
1–2 red chillies, deseeded and chopped
Salt and black pepper
1 tsp cayenne pepper

Sticky Glaze Chicken Thighs with Asian Stuffing

Place the chicken thighs in a bowl and add 40ml (3 tbsp) of the teriyaki sauce. Toss the chicken in the sauce to coat it. Cover with clingfilm (plastic wrap) and marinate in the refrigerator for at least 1 hour.

Meanwhile, make the stuffing. Mix together the ingredients in a bowl. Set aside.

Remove the chicken thighs from the marinade and pat them dry with kitchen paper (paper towels). Discard the marinade.

Preheat the oven to 200°C/400°F/gas mark 6.

Lay the chicken thighs out flat on a clean work surface. Firmly pound with the smooth side of a meat mallet to a thickness of 5mm (¼ inch). Season with salt and black pepper.

Place a chicken thigh on a piece of clingfilm. Add a spoonful of stuffing, then roll it in the clingfilm, twisting the ends to create a tight package. Repeat with the remaining chicken thighs and stuffing. Allow to rest for 10 minutes in the refrigerator.

Lay 3 pieces of string on a chopping board. Carefully unwrap a chicken thigh and lay it across the strings. Tie each string around the thigh and secure with a knot to keep the roll together. Repeat with the remaining chicken thighs.

Drizzle some rapeseed oil into a large ovenproof pan set over a medium heat. Add the rolled chicken thighs and cook for 2–3 minutes, turning regularly, to colour all sides. Transfer the pan to the oven and bake for about 25 minutes, until the centre of the chicken reaches 74°C (165°F). Transfer the chicken to a warmed plate and loosely cover it with kitchen foil.

Drain off the fat in the pan, then pour in the chicken stock, the remaining teriyaki sauce and the rice vinegar. Bring to the boil and cook over a high heat for 5–6 minutes or until the liquid has reduced by half. Remove the pan from the heat, add the butter and stir until melted. Season with salt and black pepper.

Remove the strings from chicken thighs and serve with the sauce.

Adding chorizo is a great way to inject depth and richness to savoury dishes and it combines particularly well with chicken.

SERVES 4

55g (4 tbsp) softened butter
1 tsp paprika
Salt and black pepper
1 whole chicken, about 1.6kg (3½lb)
1 small chorizo sausage, about 10cm
   (4 inches) long, finely sliced
2 tbsp olive oil
½ lemon, cut into chunks
2 garlic cloves, crushed
2 sprigs of herbs, such as rosemary,
   thyme or flat leaf parsley, plus extra
   to garnish
Lemon wedges, to garnish

Chorizo Roast Chicken

Preheat the oven to 180°C/350°F/gas mark 4.

In a bowl, combine the butter and paprika with salt and black pepper.

Run your fingers under the chicken's skin in order to detach it from the flesh, then stuff the chorizo slices and paprika butter under the skin. Now rub the chicken with olive oil.

Place the bird in a roasting pan. Put the lemon, garlic and herbs into the cavity.

Roast for 1¼ hours, basting occasionally with the chorizo butter, until the juices run clear when the thigh is pierced with a skewer or the tip of a sharp knife. Remove the roast chicken from the oven and leave it to stand for few minutes before carving. Serve sprinkled with some chopped herbs and garnished with lemon wedges.

In this dish, the meat is cooked slowly over a low heat. For a more budget-conscious dinner, you could use chicken oyster thighs in place of the jointed chicken.

SERVES 4–6

2 tbsp rapeseed (canola) oil
15g (1 tbsp) butter
1 whole chicken, about 1.6kg (3½lb), jointed into 6 or 8 pieces
Rock (kosher) salt and black pepper
175ml (¾ cup) pale ale (beer)
4 garlic cloves, crushed
3 vine tomatoes, finely chopped
Grated rind of 1 lemon
Small bunch of fresh coriander (cilantro), leaves picked and roughly chopped
100ml (½ cup) double (heavy) cream

FOR THE CRUSHED BABY POTATOES
700g (1½lb) baby potatoes
Salt and black pepper
1 tbsp olive oil
30g (2 tbsp) unsalted butter
1 tbsp chopped flat leaf parsley

FOR THE ASPARAGUS
1 tbsp olive oil
12 asparagus spears, trimmed

Chicken Fricassée with Crushed Baby Potatoes and Asparagus

Preheat the oven to 160°C/325°F/gas mark 3.

First, cook the chicken. Drizzle the oil into a large flameproof casserole dish set over a medium heat and add the butter. When foaming, sear the chicken pieces for 5–8 minutes until browned on all sides, then season with salt and black pepper.

Add the pale ale to deglaze the pan, scraping up any bits from the base of the pan. Stir to coat the chicken pieces in the beer. Bring to the boil for a few seconds, then add the garlic, tomatoes, lemon rind, coriander and cream.

Cover the pan with a lid, transfer to the oven and cook for 30 minutes. Taste and correct the seasoning if required. The chicken should be juicy and tender.

In the meantime, put the potatoes into a large saucepan of salted water, bring to the boil, then simmer for 20 minutes. Drain the potatoes, place them in a roasting pan and press lightly with a potato masher to barely open them. Drizzle over 1 tbsp of the oil, then add the seasoning, butter and parsley. Bake in the oven for roughly 40 minutes, until golden and crispy-looking.

Warm a frying pan or griddle (ridged grill) pan over a medium-high heat. Drizzle in the oil and add the asparagus. Season with salt and black pepper and cook for 3–4 minutes until the spears are caramelized and cooked through.

Serve the asparagus and crushed baby potatoes alongside the chicken.

These juicy and flavourful chicken thighs, served with delicious endive, olives and lemon rind, make a perfect brunch or supper.

SERVES 6

3 chicory (endive) bulbs
12 chicken thighs
Salt and black pepper
3 tbsp olive oil
4 onions, coarsely chopped
5 garlic cloves, finely chopped
4 tbsp white wine, such as
  Sauvignon Blanc

225ml (1 cup) warm chicken stock
225g (2¼ cups) large green olives
1 sprig of rosemary
A few sprigs of thyme
2 bay leaves
Strips of rind from 1 lemon
small handful of flat leaf parsley,
  leaves torn, to garnish

Crispy Braised Chicken Thighs with Chicory, Olives and Lemon Rind

Preheat the oven to 200°C/400°F/gas mark 6.

First, trim the bottom off the chicory bulbs and peel off and discard the first layer. Cut the bulbs into 5 x 1cm (2 x ½-inch) batons.

Season the chicken thighs on both sides with salt and black pepper.

Heat a large ovenproof pan with a little olive oil over a medium-high heat. Place the thighs in the pan, skin-side down, and brown for about 4 minutes. Turn and cook the other side for a further 3–4 minutes. Transfer the chicken pieces to a wire rack and set aside.

Reduce the heat to medium-low, add the onions to the pan and cook for 1½ minutes. Add the garlic and cook for 5 minutes, stirring often, until the onion is soft and translucent. Add the chicory and cook for 2 minutes.

Pour in the wine and chicken stock and stir in the olives, rosemary, thyme, bay leaves and strips of lemon rind and add some seasoning. Bring it all to a simmer and cook for about 2 minutes until the chicory is tender.

Return the chicken to the pan, this time with the skin-side up. When the liquid returns to a simmer, transfer the pan to the oven and cook for about 20 minutes until the chicken is cooked through.

Transfer to a serving platter and garnish with parsley leaves to serve.

I love a good chicken and ham pie, and you can add any leftover vegetables you happen to have. Puff pastry, with its light and crumbly texture, works very well in this recipe, but if you prefer a mashed-potato topping, just cook 4–6 large potatoes, mash them with a little cream, butter and seasoning and spread over the top.

SERVES 4

25g (2 tbsp) butter
1 tsp sunflower oil
4 large skinless and boneless chicken breasts, about 125–150g (4½–5½oz) each, diced
200g (1½ cups) cooked ham, diced
1 leek, trimmed and thinly sliced
1 large onion, chopped
3 garlic cloves, crushed
200g (7oz) button mushrooms
Salt and black pepper

3 tbsp plain (all-purpose) flour
150ml (¼ pint) white wine
400ml (1¾ cups) milk
55g (½ cup) smoked Gubbeen cheese or a semi-soft cows' cheese, grated
100ml (½ cup) pouring (light) cream (optional)
1 sheet of ready-rolled puff pastry, about 35 x 23cm (14 x 9 inches)
Egg wash, made with 1 egg yolk beaten with 1 tsp milk

Chicken and Ham Pie

Heat the butter and oil in a large, shallow saucepan. Add the chicken and ham and cook for 4–5 minutes. Stir in the leek, onion, garlic and mushrooms with a little seasoning and cook for 5 minutes.

Sprinkle the flour into the pan and stir to form a paste. Pour in the white wine and milk and stir in the cheese. Allow the mixture to come to a gentle boil, stirring all the time. If you like, you could add a little cream at this stage, too. Simmer for 5–6 minutes, then transfer the mixture to a large pie dish and allow it to cool for 15–20 minutes. Meanwhile, preheat the oven to 190ºC/375ºF/gas mark 5.

Cover the filling with the pastry, trimming off the excess. Crimp the edges and cut a steam-hole in the centre. Brush egg wash all over the pie and bake for about 30 minutes.

I love this dish with some nice crusty bread and a big spoonful
of fruit pickle or relish. When making a terrine, you can use most
vegetables. Nuts, such as pistachios, are also a welcome addition.

SERVES 6

6 leaves (sheets) of gelatine
500ml (2 cups) cold chicken stock
2 garlic cloves, crushed
4 tbsp flat leaf parsley, chopped
6 long baby carrots
9 asparagus spears
450g (1lb) smoked skinless and boneless
    chicken breasts (you can smoke
    chicken in a small barbecue, or
    purchase it from your butcher)
Salt and black pepper

Smoked Chicken Terrine

First, soak the gelatine in 150ml (⅔ cup) of the cold stock for about 10 minutes.

Place the remaining stock into a small saucepan. Add the garlic and parsley and
bring the stock to the boil. Remove from the heat, then add the softened gelatine
and the cold stock, stirring until the gelatine has fully dissolved. Set aside, but
don't allow the stock to set – you have about 30 minutes in which to prepare the
remaining part of the terrine.

Blanch the carrots and asparagus in boiling water for 2–3 minutes. Remove from
the pan and place in iced water to stop the cooking process.

Line a 900g (9 x 5 x 3-inch) loaf tin with clingfilm (plastic wrap) so that it overhangs
the sides of the tin. Ensure the clingfilm is not pierced and that it is fully pressed
into the corners of the tin. Pour a thin layer of stock into the bottom of the tin. Place
3 of the asparagus spears in the bottom, then arrange about half of the chicken
on top, tearing the pieces to fit. Season this layer with salt and black pepper (and
continue to season the layers as you work). Place 3 carrots on top of the chicken,
then pour over half of the remaining chicken stock. Repeat by adding a further
layer of 3 asparagus spears, the remaining chicken, then 3 carrots, then pour over
the remaining stock. Place the remaining 3 asparagus spears on top. Fold over the
clingfilm and refrigerate overnight.

To serve, invert the terrine onto a serving plate and remove the clingfilm.

When smoking your own turkey crown, it's essential that you have a meat thermometer to ensure it reaches the correct temperature of 74°C (165°F). When smoked, the turkey will appear different from a traditional oven-roasted bird, being pink and having a smoother finish.

SERVES 6–8

150g (1½ sticks) butter, melted
2 garlic cloves, crushed
Salt and black pepper
3 tbsp chopped rosemary
3 tbsp chopped thyme
1 turkey crown (breast), about
  5.5kg (12lb)
2–3 tbsp olive oil

FOR THE FIG AND ORANGE SALAD
2 tbsp orange juice
2 tbsp olive oil
1 tbsp white wine vinegar
2 oranges, peeled, segmented and
  membrane removed
3–4 figs, cut into wedges
4 spring onions (scallions), chopped
200g (7oz) watercress
2 tbsp pine nuts, toasted

Smoked Turkey with Fig and Orange Salad

Mix together the melted butter, garlic, salt, black pepper and herbs in a small bowl. Rub the turkey crown with the mixture and drizzle with the olive oil.

My preference for cooking this recipe is with a kettle barbecue, because it is important that the turkey is covered with a lid during cooking. You can use a variety of woodchips to smoke the meat. Make sure they have been presoaked in cider, fruit juice or wine for at least 30 minutes before adding them to the coals.

Allow about 35 minutes of cooking time per 450g (1 lb) of turkey. Add extra woodchips or charcoal every hour until the turkey is cooked. When it is ready, remove it from the barbecue and allow it to rest, covered in foil, for at least 30 minutes.

Meanwhile, whisk together the orange juice, olive oil, white wine vinegar and some salt and black pepper in a small bowl.

Put the orange segments, figs, spring onions, watercress and half the pine nuts into a large salad bowl. Pour over the salad dressing and toss gently to combine.

Carve the smoked turkey into slices and place along one side of a large platter. Arrange the salad alongside the turkey and scatter over the remaining pine nuts.

There is something wonderfully satisfying about putting a beautiful turkey in the middle of the table on Christmas Day and serving your waiting family. If cooked properly, it can be a deliciously moist bird, so follow my method below. My other tip is to plan every aspect of your Christmas cookery meticulously, then you can relax a little more on the actual day.

SERVES 8–10

250g (2¼ sticks) butter
3 tbsp chopped sage
1 whole turkey, about 6.5kg (14¼lb)
Salt and black pepper
400g (14oz) Chestnut, Cranberry
   and Sausagemeat Stuffing (see
    page 152)
400g (14oz) Sage and Onion Stuffing
   (see page 152)
Turkey Gravy (see page 207), to serve

Kevin's Christmas Turkey

Preheat the oven to 180°C/350°F/gas mark 4.

First, soften the butter in a bowl, add the sage and mix well. Rub the sage butter underneath the turkey-breast skin by lifting the skin gently with your hands and massaging the butter onto the flesh. Season with some salt and black pepper.

Pack the sausagemeat stuffing into the neck cavity, then line the main cavity with some kitchen foil or nonstick baking paper and loosely pack the sage stuffing into the bird. Don't forget to weigh the turkey with the stuffing enclosed so that you can plan your cooking time accordingly. Allow 20 minutes per 450g (1lb), then an additional 20–30 minutes in the oven. In total, it should take about 5½–6 hours.

Put the turkey into a large roasting pan, cover with kitchen foil and place it in the oven for 2 hours. Remove the foil and continue roasting, basting occasionally, for the remaining time. To check that the turkey is cooked, insert a skewer or the tip of sharp knife into the leg meat nearest the bone, the juices should run completely clear when the turkey is ready.

Cover the bird with foil and allow to rest for at least 30 minutes when it comes out of the oven, then carve as required. Serve with the stuffings and the gravy.

'Chicken with a slightly gamey taste' is the way I describe the flavour of pheasant, and adding bacon makes a mouth-watering combination. Cook the meat in batches to prevent overcrowding the pan and steaming rather than sealing the meat. If preferred, add some Guinness rather than wine.

SERVES 4–6

2 tbsp plain (all-purpose) flour
Salt and black pepper
1 pheasant, about 900g (2lb),
    skinned and cut into portions
2 tbsp sunflower oil
150g (5½oz) bacon lardons
    (diced bacon)
1 onion, sliced
1 bay leaf
2–3 sprigs of thyme
150g (5½oz) button mushrooms
250ml (1 cup) red wine
250ml (1 cup) chicken or beef stock

Pheasant and Bacon Casserole

Season the flour with some salt and black pepper, then spread it on a plate. Toss the pheasant in the flour, then gently pat to remove any excess.

Heat the oil in a frying pan and fry the pheasant in batches until sealed, then transfer to a flameproof casserole dish.

Fry the bacon, onion, herbs and mushrooms for 2–3 minutes until the bacon begins to colour. Transfer the mixture to the casserole dish.

Pour in the wine and stock, season with salt and black pepper, then bring to the boil. Reduce the heat and simmer for 1½–2 hours. Discard the thyme and bay leaf. Season to taste and serve with some creamy mashed potatoes.

I like to serve with this wild duck dish with a crispy Potato Rösti (see page 160).

SERVES 6

6 mallard or duck breasts
Oil, for frying

FOR THE STUFFING
140g (1¼ sticks) butter
½ onion, chopped
2 tbsp chopped mixed herbs, such as thyme, rosemary, parsley and sage
225g (5 cups) fresh breadcrumbs
100g (3½oz) cold mashed potato
Salt and black pepper
85g (¾ cup) walnuts

FOR THE RED WINE AND PLUM REDUCTION
25g (2 tbsp) butter
2 shallots, sliced
3 garlic cloves, chopped
2 sprigs of thyme
85g (½ cup) plums, stoned (pitted) and diced
4 tbsp dark brown sugar
600ml (2½ cups) red wine
1 tsp tomato purée (paste)
3 tbsp port

Pan-seared Mallard with a Crunchy Walnut Stuffing and Red Wine and Plum Reduction

First make the reduction. In a large frying pan, melt the butter and add the shallots, garlic, thyme and plums. Glaze quickly until everything begins to soften slightly. Next, add the brown sugar and allow this to melt and bubble up around the sides of the saucepan. This will give a nice sweet flavour to the sauce, which makes a perfect accompaniment to the mallard. Reduce the heat to quite low and pour in the red wine, tomato purée and port. Allow this mixture to come to a gentle boil, then heat for about 25 minutes until reduced to a syrupy consistency. Keep warm.

Next, make the stuffing. In a large saucepan, melt the butter on a medium-low heat and fry the onion for 4–5 minutes. Add the chopped herbs and breadcrumbs. Transfer the mixture to a bowl and allow it to cool. Stir in the mashed potato, some seasoning and the walnuts.

Heat a large frying pan with a tiny amount of oil. Lay the mallard breasts on a chopping board or a serving plate and season with a little salt and black pepper. Pan-fry them for 4–5 minutes on each side until crispy and golden brown.

Allow the breasts to rest for 5 minutes, then serve on top of the crunchy walnut stuffing with the reduction drizzled over.

The duck breasts from Skeaghanore in County Cork have a full flavour and succulent taste, which comes from being hand-reared for longer and being fed a natural cereal-based diet. They make a superlative dish, but any duck breasts will work well in this recipe.

SERVES 4

2 duck breasts
Salt and black pepper
3 tbsp honey
Juice of ½ lemon
200g (1 cup) canned cherries,
    preferably Amarena
25ml (1 shot) Kirsch liqueur (optional)

Skeaghanore Duck Breasts with Black Cherries

Slit the breasts on the skin side in a grid pattern without cutting into the flesh. Season with a little salt and black pepper.

Place a heavy-based frying pan over a high heat and, when the pan is really hot, put in the duck breasts with the skin-side facing down. This will allow the fat to melt and the skin to crisp up.

Cook for about 5 minutes on each side over a medium heat, ensuring you regularly drain off the fat during cooking. Transfer the duck to a warmed plate, cover with kitchen foil and keep warm.

Add the honey, lemon juice, 2 tbsp of the cherry juice and the Kirsch, if using. Bring the mixture to a simmer, scraping up any bits stuck to the base of the pan, and then reduce it by half. Stir in the cherries.

Coat the duck breasts in the sauce and serve immediately with some Sautéed Garlic Potatoes (see page 160).

'Confit' is a French word that describes the way meat is cooked and preserved in its own fat. In this dish, the process creates gently cured duck legs, slowly cooked to falling-off-the-bone perfection.

SERVES 4

Oil, for frying
4 duck legs, about 175g (6oz) each
1kg (2¼lb) jar of duck fat
2 bay leaves
2–3 juniper berries
3–4 sprigs of thyme

FOR THE BLACKCURRANT JUS
1 tbsp oil
2 shallots, finely chopped
1 carrot, finely chopped

4 rashers (slices) of bacon, chopped
1 tbsp chopped thyme leaves
Salt and black pepper
85g (1 cup) blackcurrants
400ml (1¾ cups) red wine
350ml (1½ cups) warm beef stock

FOR THE CARROT AND CUMIN PURÉE
4 large carrots, roughly chopped
200ml (1 cup) milk
1 tsp ground cumin
4 tbsp double (heavy) cream,
  heated

Confit of Duck Leg with Carrot and Cumin Purée and Blackcurrant Jus

Preheat the oven to 150°C/300°F/gas mark 2. Put a large roasting pan on the hob or stove over a medium heat. Using a little oil, fry the duck legs, skin-side down, for about 5 minutes. Once browned, add in the duck fat, bay leaves, juniper berries and thyme sprigs and transfer to the oven for 1½ hours. When cooked, place the duck legs on a wire rack for 5 minutes to allow the fat to drain off.

Make the blackcurrant jus. Heat the oil in a large saucepan over a medium heat. Add the shallots, carrot, bacon, thyme, salt and black pepper and cook until the bacon is well browned. Add in the blackcurrants and red wine and bring to the boil. Add in about two-thirds of the stock and bring back to the boil. Reduce the heat and simmer for about 20 minutes. Add the additional stock as necessary to prevent the sauce from becoming too concentrated in either texture or flavour. Strain through a fine sieve or strainer, then return to a simmer for an additional 10 minutes.

In the meantime, make the purée. Place the carrots in a large saucepan with the milk and bring to the boil. Reduce the heat and allow the mixture to simmer until the carrot has softened. Strain off 90 per cent of the liquid and transfer the remainder and the carrots to a food processor. Add the ground cumin and cream and blitz until very smooth.

To serve, put a spoonful of the purée in the centre of each plate and place a duck leg on it. Drizzle a little jus over both and serve immediately.

The flavour of venison is wonderful in this dish. The fillet is poached in a red wine stock, which makes a welcome change from the usual venison stews, and is the perfect winter warmer.

SERVES 4

800g (1¾lb) venison fillet, deveined

FOR THE POACHING STOCK
300ml (1¼ cups) red wine
250ml (1 cup) venison stock
2 cinnamon sticks
4 cardamom seeds
2 cloves
1 orange, quartered

FOR THE CRANBERRY JUS
200ml (1 cup) warm venison or beef
  stock
Grated rind of 1 orange
50g (½ cup) cranberries

Fillet of Venison Poached in Mulled Wine with a Cranberry Jus

Roll the venison fillet tightly in clingfilm (plastic wrap) to give it a cylindrical shape. Set it aside in a cold room.

Now prepare the poaching stock. Pour the red wine and venison stock into a deep pan and add the spices and orange pieces. Bring the mixture to the boil, then simmer for 15 minutes.

Unwrap the venison fillet and poach it in the simmering liquid for about 18–20 minutes.

Meanwhile, to make the cranberry jus, put 200ml (1 cup) of poaching stock into a saucepan, add the venison or beef stock and the orange zest and bring to the boil. Reduce the heat and simmer until the liquid has reduced by half and coats the back of a spoon without being runny. Add the cranberries to the jus during the last few minutes of the venison poaching time.

Remove the venison from the poaching stock and toss it quickly in the cranberry jus to give it a glossy look.

Place the venison on a board and slice into 4 equal portions. Serve with Roasted Butternut Squash Mousseline (see page 150), accompanied by a sauceboat of the cranberry jus.

Wood pigeon is a small game bird that is high in protein and, thanks to the diversity of its wild diet (seeds, acorns, buds, berries and green crops), it has a wonderfully complex woodland taste. It's the basis of the perfect autumnal salad.

SERVES 4

Sunflower oil, for frying
2 parsnips, cut into ribbons with a
  mandoline or potato peeler
Salt and black pepper
2 tsp curry powder
50g (4 tbsp) butter
4 wood pigeon breasts

100g (3½oz) very thin rashers (slices)
  of smoked bacon
4 tbsp white balsamic or sherry vinegar
200g (7oz) salad leaves or greens

FOR THE DRESSING
Juice of 1 lemon
1 garlic clove, crushed
4 tbsp olive oil

Wood Pigeon Salad with Curried Parsnip Crisps

Heat some sunflower oil to 140°C (285°F) in a large saucepan or deep-fat fryer. Deep-fry the parsnip strips for about 5 minutes until crisp and golden brown. Transfer them to a bowl lined with kitchen paper (paper towels). Sprinkle with salt and curry powder and set aside.

Prepare the dressing. Put the lemon juice, garlic and olive oil into a small bowl and season with salt and black pepper. Mix well.

Heat a pan over a high heat until it's hot, then drizzle in 1 tbsp sunflower oil and add the butter. When it foams, add the pigeon breasts and season well with salt and black pepper. Cook them for about 90 seconds on each side, then remove and set aside.

Tip the excess oil out of the pan, then add the bacon. Fry for a couple of minutes, then remove and drain it on kitchen paper. Set aside.

Put the pan back on the heat and pour in the balsamic vinegar. Reduce this to about 2 tbsp of liquid, then return the pigeon breasts to the pan and coat them in the sauce.

Place the salad leaves in a bowl and drizzle with the dressing. Mix well and season with salt and black pepper. Place a handful of salad in the middle of 4 large plates and dot the bacon around the edges. Slice the warm pigeon breasts into about 6 thin slices (the flesh should be pink throughout) and lay them on top of the salad leaves. Drizzle over some reduction from the pan and place a few parsnip crisps (chips) on top. Serve immediately.

Meat

This comforting broth has the flavour of home at Easter to me. You'll need brisket or silverside for this recipe, and the cooking process is long and slow, but it makes the meat tender and juicy.

SERVES 4–6

1.5kg (3¼lb) corned beef silverside (bottom round), cut in half
250ml (1 cup) beer
2 oranges, halved
1 garlic bulb, crushed
1 bay leaf
2 sprigs of thyme
4 tbsp honey
4 tbsp sherry vinegar
1 tsp mustard seeds
3 star anise
2 tsp black peppercorns
500ml (2 cups) water
1 onion, cut into wedges

500g (1lb 2oz) potatoes (or 4 potatoes), quartered
500g (1lb 2oz) baby carrots (or 4 carrots cut into batons about 6cm/2½ inches long)
200g (7oz) baby turnips (or ¼ large turnip cut into small chunks)
1 small head of cabbage, about 300g (10½oz), cut into wedges

Pulled Corned Beef

Place the beef in a large saucepan with the beer, oranges, garlic, bay leaf, thyme sprigs, honey, vinegar, spices and peppercorns and cover with water. Put a lid on the pan and bring to the boil, then reduce the heat and simmer for about 2½–3 hours, topping up the water during cooking if necessary, until a fork can be easily inserted into the centre of the meat. Carefully remove the beef and put it on a cutting board to rest for about for 10 minutes.

Add the 500ml (2 cups) of water to the pan and bring to the boil over a medium heat. Put in the vegetables and bring back up to the boil. Reduce the heat to a low simmer and cook for 15–20 minutes until the vegetables are tender. Discard the orange pieces.

Use 2 forks to pull the meat apart. Divide it between bowls and serve with the broth and vegetables.

The flavour of beef cooked on the bone is far superior to that cooked off the bone. Ensure you allow the meat to rest for as long as possible before carving. The horseradish sauce can be stored in the refrigerator for up to 2 days.

SERVES 4

2 carrots, roughly chopped
1 large onion, roughly chopped
1 sprig of rosemary
Olive oil
2 ribs of beef (on the bone), about
    450g (1lb) each
400g (14oz) baby (pearl) onions
4 tbsp water
50g (4 tbsp) butter
1 tbsp granulated sugar
Salt and black pepper

FOR THE HORSERADISH CREAM
100ml (½ cup) double (heavy) cream
1 tbsp malt vinegar
50g (¾ cup) horseradish, grated

Rib of Beef with Baby Onions and Horseradish Cream

Preheat the oven to 200°C/400°F/gas mark 6.

Put the roughly chopped carrots, onion and sprig of rosemary into a roasting pan to make a bed for the meat, then set aside.

Select a large frying pan, add a little olive oil and place it over a high heat. Sear the ribs of beef for 3 minutes on each side, then transfer to the roasting pan on top of the vegetables. Roast in the oven for 20–25 minutes for medium-rare meat and over 30 minutes for well done.

Meanwhile, place the baby onions in a pan, pour in the water and add the butter. Stir in the sugar and season with salt and black pepper. Bring to the boil, then simmer for 5–10 minutes until the water has evaporated and the onions are slightly caramelized.

To make the horseradish cream, place the cream in a large bowl with the vinegar and whisk until soft peaks are formed. Fold in the horseradish and season with salt and black pepper.

To serve, place the ribs of beef on a wooden board or large serving dish and carve at the table. Serve with Horseradish Dauphinoise Potatoes (see page 162) and offer the baby onions and horseradish sauce separately.

Guinness (or stout) will not only help tenderize the stewing beef, but it also adds a lovely malty flavour to this robust pie.

SERVES 4

2 tbsp olive oil
30g (2 tbsp) butter
675g (1½lb) stewing beef (boneless beef chuck), cut into 2.5cm (1 inch) cubes
Salt and black pepper
2 large onions, sliced
2 garlic cloves, chopped
150g (2 cups) mushrooms. sliced
2 sprigs of thyme
3 tbsp plain (all-purpose) flour

2 tsp tomato purée (paste)
2 tsp Worcestershire sauce
500ml (2 cups) Guinness
300ml (1¼ cups) warm beef stock
Egg wash, made with 1 egg yolk beaten with 1 tsp milk

FOR THE PASTRY
225g (1¾ cups) plain (all-purpose) flour
Pinch of salt
115g (½ cup) shredded suet (or equal parts butter and lard, chopped)
2–3 tbsp cold water

Beef and Guinness Pie

Preheat the oven to 150°C/300°F/gas mark 2.

Drizzle the olive oil into a frying pan set over a medium heat and add a knob or pat of butter. Add the meat to the pan in batches and fry for about 2–3 minutes on each side. Transfer to an ovenproof casserole dish. Season the meat with salt and black pepper.

Add the remaining butter to the frying pan, then add the onions, garlic, mushrooms and thyme and cook for 3–5 minutes until the onion is translucent. Sprinkle over the flour, then add the tomato purée and Worcestershire sauce and cook for about 2 minutes. Pour in the stout and warm beef stock and stir well.

Pour the contents of the pan into the casserole dish, cover with a tight-fitting lid and transfer to the oven. Cook for 2 hours, checking occasionally to ensure there is enough liquid in the casserole dish and adding a little water if necessary. Once cooked, allow to cool for 30 minutes.

Meanwhile, make the pastry. Sift the flour into a large bowl and add the salt. Add the suet and just enough water to bind the ingredients and make a soft but not sticky dough. Wrap the dough in clingfilm (plastic wrap) and place in the refrigerator for 20 minutes.

Roll out the pastry on a lightly floured work surface and use it to line 4 individual pie dishes. Reroll the offcuts, then, using the top of a dish as a template, cut out 4 lids. Chill the lined pie dishes and pastry lids for 20 minutes. Preheat the oven to 200°C/400°F/gas mark 6.

Fill the pastry cases with the meat and brush the edges with the egg wash. Place the lids on the pies, crimp the edges to seal, then brush the lids with the egg wash. Pierce a steam-hole in the centre of each and bake for 30–35 minutes until the pastry is crisp and golden.

If you are not a garlic fan, add some grated cheese or snipped chives to the mashed potato – or sometimes plain and simple buttery mash just hits the spot.

SERVES 4–6

1 tbsp olive oil
2 onions, finely chopped
3–4 celery sticks, finely chopped
2 small carrots, finely chopped
4 garlic cloves, crushed
1 tsp chopped thyme
750g (1¾lb) minced (ground) beef
2 tsp tomato purée (paste)
200ml (1 cup) red wine or 150ml
   (⅔ cup) beef stock
1 tbsp Worcestershire sauce (optional)

FOR THE GARLIC MASH
1 garlic bulb
Olive oil
6–8 potatoes, chopped
25g (2 tbsp) butter
3 tbsp milk
Salt and black pepper

Roasted Garlic Cottage Pie

Preheat the oven to 190°C/375°C/gas mark 5.

First make the mash. Horizontally slice the bulb of garlic. Place it in kitchen foil, drizzle with a little oil, then seal tightly and bake in the oven for 45–55 minutes until the garlic has softened.

Put the potatoes into a large saucepan of water and bring to the boil. Reduce the heat and simmer for about 20 minutes until the potatoes are softened. Strain into a large colander and return them to the saucepan with the butter and milk. Squeeze in the roasted garlic and season with salt and black pepper. Mash the potatoes until completely smooth.

While the potatoes and garlic are cooking, make the pie filling. Heat the olive oil in a frying pan. Add the onions, celery, carrots, garlic and thyme and sauté for 3–4 minutes until the onion is just beginning to soften but has not yet coloured. Stir the meat into the pan and cook for 5–6 minutes until browned, breaking up any lumps with the back of a wooden spoon. Stir in the tomato purée and the red wine or stock and cook gently for another 15–20 minutes until completely tender. Add in the Worcestershire sauce, if using.

Place the beef in an ovenproof casserole dish. Pipe or spoon the mashed potato on the top of the meat mixture.

Bake for 20–25 minutes until the filling is bubbling hot and the topping is golden brown. Serve immediately with some crisp green vegetables.

If you are trying to impress or satisfy, steak is always the answer. I like to serve this steak and its accompanying salad with some Thick Hand-cut Chips (see page 165).

SERVES 4

800g (1¾lb) fillet of beef (tenderloin), trimmed
1 tbsp olive oil
200g (7oz) mixed salad leaves or greens
200g (1⅓ cups) Cashel Blue Cheese, crumbled
1 orange, peeled, segmented and membrane removed
½ pink grapefruit, peeled, segmented and membrane removed
Salt and black pepper

Pan-seared Fillet of Beef with a Lively Cashel Blue Cheese Salad

Preheat the oven to 200°C/400°F/gas mark 6.

Slice the beef into medallions that are about 2.5–4cm (1–1½ inches) thick.

Heat a frying pan until smoking hot, then brush with the oil and sear the medallions for about 1–2 minutes on each side. Transfer to a baking sheet and cook in the oven: 5 minutes for a rare steak, 8 minutes for medium-rare and 15 minutes for well done.

Remove the steaks from the oven, allow to rest for a few minutes, then carve them into thick slices.

To serve, divide half the salad leaves between 4 plates. Top with slices of steak, scatter around the blue cheese and citrus segments, season with salt and black pepper and top with the remaining salad leaves.

When I get out the barbecue to and make these burgers, I ensure I have plenty of napkins to hand, not only to clear up around me as I cook, but also to mop up the meaty juices that escape with each mouthful. These tender burgers will definitely be a hit with your guests, especially if you serve them with a delicious Red Onion Marmalade (see page 215).

SERVES 8

700g (1½lb) lean minced (ground) beef
2 spring onions (scallions), finely chopped
2 garlic cloves, finely chopped
55g (1¼ cups) fresh breadcrumbs
55g (½ cup) Wexford or any good vintage Cheddar, grated
2–4 tsp chopped herbs (such as parsley or thyme)
2 tsp tomato ketchup or sweet chilli jam (optional)
Pinch of ground cinnamon
Salt and black pepper
1 large (US extra-large) egg

Plain (all-purpose) flour, for dusting
1 tbsp olive oil

TO SERVE
8 Caramelized Onion Bread Rolls (see page 36)
Olive oil, for drizzling
Slices of Wexford vintage Cheddar cheese (or use any good vintage Cheddar)
Red Onion Marmalade (see page 215)
Cherry tomatoes, halved
Rashers (slices) of streaky (fatty) bacon, grilled
Mixed salad leaves or greens

Kevin's Classic Beef Burger

Light the barbecue. Put the beef into a large mixing bowl and add in the spring onions and garlic. Mix in the breadcrumbs, grated cheese and chopped herbs, together with the tomato ketchup and cinnamon. Season the mixture with a little salt and black pepper. Add in the egg and combine the mixture with your hands – the egg will act as a binding agent.

Divide the mixture into 8 equal pieces and, using a little plain flour to reduce stickiness, shape them into patties about 1cm (½ inch) thick. Place the patties on a baking sheet and leave them to rest in the refrigerator for at least 30 minutes.

Brush the burgers with a little oil, place them on the barbecue rack and cook on each side for 4–5 minutes. (Alternatively, place the sheet of burgers in an oven preheated to 180°C/350°F/gas mark 4 for 8–10 minutes until they are fully cooked.)

In the meantime, split the bread rolls in half, drizzle the cut sides with olive oil and toast them lightly on the barbecue. Immediately add the burgers, then encourage your guests to build their own burgers with the cheese slices, red onion marmalade, tomatoes, bacon and mixed salad leaves.

This dish involves a lot of preparation but will impress your guests with its simplicity and flavour!

SERVES 6

2 litres (5 cups) warm beef stock
1.4 litres (6 cups) red wine
1 sprig of rosemary
2 sprigs of thyme
1 bay leaf
2½ tbsp flour
Salt and black pepper
2kg (4½lb) oxtail, cut into pieces
100g (1 stick) butter
2 tbsp rapeseed (canola) oil

5 shallots, chopped
½ garlic bulb, crushed
2 large onions, finely chopped
2 carrots, diced
1 tsp tomato purée (paste)
1 celery stick with leaves, finely chopped
2 tbsp chopped flat leaf parsley
6 sheets of fresh egg lasagne or noodles
1 tsp olive oil
200g (1⅓ cups) peas, blanched
15g (¾ cup) chervil sprigs

Oxtail Open Ravioli

Preheat the oven to 160°C/325°F/gas mark 3.

Place the beef stock, red wine and herbs in a saucepan and bring to the boil. Simmer until the liquid has reduced by about one-third.

Meanwhile, combine the flour and salt and black pepper in a large bowl. Dredge the oxtail in the seasoned flour, then shake off the excess. Set aside.

In a large flameproof casserole dish, heat 20g (1½ tbsp) of the butter with 1 tbsp of the oil over a medium-low heat. Brown the oxtail on all sides, in batches if necessary, which will take about 10 minutes. Remove the oxtail from the casserole and set aside.

Increase the heat to medium and add another 20g (1½ tbsp) of the butter to the casserole dish. Stir in the shallots, garlic, onions, carrots, tomato purée, celery and parsley. Cook, stirring, for 8–10 minutes until the vegetables have softened. Pour in the reduced beef stock, add the caramelized oxtail and bring to the boil.

Cover the casserole with a tight-fitting lid or foil, then place in the oven for 3–4 hours until the oxtail is very tender and nearly falling off the bone. Check occasionally to ensure there is enough liquid in the casserole dish and add a little water if necessary.

Transfer the meat to a dish and leave it to cool. Strain the remaining braising liquid through a fine-mesh sieve or strainer into a clean saucepan. Set aside the cooked vegetables. Simmer the braising liquid over a medium heat until it has reduced to about 575ml (2⅓ cups). Whisk in the remaining butter. Keep warm until required.

Ease the oxtail off the bone and chop quite small. Place it in a bowl, add the cooked vegetables and a drizzle of the sauce and keep warm until needed.

Bring a large saucepan of salted water to the boil. Add the lasagne sheets, stir and bring the water back to the boil. Reduce the heat so the water is simmering and cook the pasta for 10–12 minutes, or as per the package instructions, until al dente. Drain well and drizzle with the olive oil.

Add the peas and chervil to the sauce. Taste and adjust the seasoning if necessary.

To serve, set out 6 warmed pasta bowls and place a drained lasagne sheet in each one. Top with the oxtail mixture, then wrap the sheet around it. Spoon over the pea sauce and serve immediately.

Sometimes I double the mixture for this recipe to make meatballs, which I serve with a delicious tomato sauce. Just add a can of chopped tomatoes to some fried onion and garlic, heat to thicken, then add seasoning and a few torn basil leaves.

SERVES 4

20g (1½ tbsp) butter
10 rashers (slices) of bacon
1 onion, finely diced
1 carrot, finely diced
½ celery stick, finely diced
Olive oil
500g (1lb 2oz) lean minced (ground) beef
4 garlic cloves, chopped
140g (3 cups) fresh breadcrumbs
2 tbsp tomato purée (paste)
1 tsp Worcestershire sauce
1 tsp Dijon mustard
1 tbsp chopped flat leaf parsley or oregano
Salt and black pepper
1 egg, beaten

FOR THE GARLIC MASH
900g (2lb) Rooster or Yukon Gold potatoes (or 8 potatoes), cut into large chunks
1 garlic bulb, roasted (see page 96)
50g (2 tbsp) butter

Mum's Meatloaf

Preheat the oven to 190°C/375°F/gas mark 5.

Prepare a 500g (8½ x 4½ x 2½-inch) loaf tin by greasing it with the butter, then line it with the bacon, letting the ends overhang the tin.

Heat a little oil in a frying pan set over a medium heat. Add the onion, carrot and celery and fry until softened. Remove from the heat and leave to cool down for several minutes.

Place the beef in a large bowl, add the carrot mixture, the garlic, breadcrumbs, tomato purée, Worcestershire sauce, mustard, herbs, salt, pepper and egg and mix well. Spoon into the tin, smooth the surface and fold the bacon over it. Cover the tin with kitchen foil and bake for 1–1¼ hours. Remove the foil for the last 15 minutes of cooking.

Meanwhile, make the garlic mashed potato. Put the potatoes in a large saucepan, barely cover them with water and boil for about 25 minutes until they are very tender but not falling apart. Drain and return them to the saucepan over a low heat, then roughly mash. Squeeze in the roasted garlic, add the butter and beat with a wooden spoon until the potato is fluffy. Season with salt and black pepper and keep warm.

Allow the meatloaf to sit for 10 minutes before removing it from the tin. Serve hot or cold, cut into slices, with the garlic mash.

Bookmaker's Sandwich

This sandwich is so named because, traditionally, it is taken to the racecourse and will fill you up for the day. The juices from the steak ooze through the bread, making a moist, satisfying sandwich. You can add some fried onions and mushrooms if you wish. Just cook them in a little garlic butter and layer them on top of the steak – delicious!

SERVES 4

1 tbsp olive oil
650–700g (1½lb) sirloin (tenderloin) or striploin (strip) steak
1 loaf of crusty bread (such as a Vienna loaf), about 500g (1lb 2oz)
40g (3 tbsp) butter
2–3 tsp Dalkey mustard (or use wholegrain mustard)
Salt and black pepper

Place a frying pan over a high heat and drizzle in the oil. Add the steak and cook for 2–3 minutes on each side (depending on thickness) for medium-rare. Ensure you do not overcook the steak.

In the meantime, slice the loaf in half lengthways and spread butter on one side and mustard on the other. Place the steak on top. Season with some salt and black pepper.

Sandwich the loaf back together and wrap it in some nonstick baking paper. Place a weight, such as a saucepan, on top of the loaf and allow the juices to penetrate through the bread for 5–8 minutes.

Insert a wooden skewer or toothpick to hold the slices in place and cut the loaf vertically into thick slices. Serve on a plate and enjoy at your leisure.

Flank Steak with Confit Shallots

Flank steaks are best cooked medium to rare – they become too tough if well done. To accompany this dish, I recommend the baked Hasselback Potatoes (see page 166).

SERVES 2

40g (3 tbsp) butter
4 shallots, sliced
1 tbsp balsamic vinegar
2 tbsp caster (superfine) sugar
100ml (½ cup) red wine
1 tbsp rapeseed (canola) oil
2 flank steaks (or striploin/strip steaks), about 225g (8oz) each
Salt and black pepper

Melt half the butter in a small saucepan and sauté the shallots over a low heat for about 4–6 minutes. Add the balsamic vinegar and sugar to deglaze the pan, scraping up any bits from the base of the pan. Add the red wine, reduce the heat to medium-low and simmer for about 5–8 minutes, stirring occasionally. The sauce should reduce considerably; at the end, it will have lost half its volume and have a glossy texture.

In a large frying pan over a high heat, melt the remaining butter with the rapeseed oil, add the flank steaks, season well and cook for a 2–3 minutes on each side. Transfer to warmed serving plates and drizzle over the sauce. Serve immediately.

The red wine reduction really enhances the flavour of the lamb – make sure you use a good-quality wine that you would drink. Try adding a spoonful of redcurrant jelly to the reduction for some extra depth of flavour.

SERVES 4–6

1.5–2kg (3¼–4½lb) leg of lamb
2–3 garlic cloves, sliced
2–3 sprigs of rosemary
Salt and black pepper

FOR THE RED WINE REDUCTION
1–2 shallots, finely diced
1 tsp olive oil
300ml (1¼ cups) red wine
300ml (1¼ cups) beef stock
1 tsp chopped rosemary
Knob or pat of butter

Roast Leg of Lamb with a Red Wine Reduction

Preheat the oven to 220°C/425°F/gas mark 7.

Place the leg of lamb in a large roasting pan. Make some deep incisions in the meat and insert slices of garlic and small rosemary sprigs. Season well with salt and black pepper.

Place the lamb on the top shelf of the oven and roast for 1½–1¾ hours. Set aside to rest, covered with kitchen foil, for 10 minutes before thinly slicing it.

In a small saucepan over a medium heat, sauté the shallots in the olive oil until they are translucent but not browned. Add the red wine, beef stock, seasoning and rosemary and cook until the liquid has reduced by half. Add the butter to the sauce to create a glossy finish.

Serve slices of the lamb on a bed of Boulangère Potatoes (see page 162), drizzled with a little red wine reduction and accompanied by garden peas.

Fall-off-the-bone meat is one of my favourite things. Here slowly cooked lamb shanks are served with cannellini beans to absorb the wonderful meat juices.

SERVES 4

50g (⅓ cup) plain (all-purpose) flour
Salt and black pepper
4 lamb shanks, about 400g (14oz)
  each
2 tbsp olive oil
18 baby (pearl) onions
3 carrots, cut into chunks
4 garlic cloves, chopped
1 tsp tomato purée
4 tomatoes, cut into quarters
250g (1¼ cups) dried cannellini beans,
  presoaked and drained

1 bunch of thyme
1 bay leaf
2–3 sprigs of rosemary
300ml (1¼ cups) red wine
500ml (2 cups) chicken or lamb stock

Braised Lamb Shanks with Cannellini Beans

Preheat the oven 140°C/275°F/gas mark 1.

Season the flour with some salt and black pepper, then spread it out on a plate. Toss the lamb shanks in the flour.

Heat the olive oil in a large frying pan and fry the lamb shanks over a high heat, cooking for 8–10 minutes and turning regularly until the meat is coloured on all sides. Remove the meat from the pan and transfer to a large ovenproof casserole dish.

Keeping the heat high, add the onions and carrots to the empty pan and brown these as well, turning and tossing them around for 3–4 minutes.

Add the seasoned flour left over after coating the lamb and stir until it has darkened in colour.

Now stir in the garlic and tomato purée, cook for 1 minute, then add the tomatoes, the drained beans and herbs and stir to combine. Pour the wine and stock into the pan, bring to the boil. Pour into the casserole dish and cover with a lid. Place in the oven for about 2½–3 hours until the meat is tender, checking occasionally to ensure there is enough liquid in the casserole dish and adding a little water if necessary.

A shoulder of lamb takes a long time to become tender, which is why it is the perfect choice for slow roasting.

SERVES 4–6

2kg (4½lb) shoulder of lamb
8–10 sprigs of rosemary
8–10 sprigs of thyme
1 garlic bulb, ½ crushed and
    ½ chopped
Grated rind and juice of 2 lemons
Salt and black pepper
4 tbsp olive oil

1 tbsp plain (all-purpose) flour
200ml (1 cup) red wine
500ml (2 cups) lamb stock
2 tbsp capers, drained and chopped
½ lemon, peeled and segmented

Slow-roasted Shoulder of Wexford Lamb with Rosemary and Thyme

Preheat the oven to 220°C/425°F/gas mark 7.

Score the fat side of the lamb shoulder with a sharp knife.

Scatter half the sprigs of rosemary and thyme in a large roasting pan, then add the crushed garlic.

In a small bowl, combine the lemon juice and rind, chopped garlic and some salt and black pepper. Drizzle some of this mixture over the lamb and rub in thoroughly. Season well and then place the meat in the roasting pan. Tear the remaining sprigs of rosemary and thyme into 2.5 cm (1-inch) pieces and sprinkle over the lamb.

Roast for 15 minutes, then cover with kitchen foil, reduce the heat to 160°C/325°F/gas mark 3 and cook for 4 hours.

Remove it from the oven and allow to rest, still covered in kitchen foil, for 10–15 minutes before serving.

To make the jus, remove most of the fat from the roasting pan, place it on the hob or stove and mix in the flour. Add the wine and scrape up all the gooeyness from the bottom of the tin. Add the stock and the chopped capers and simmer for a couple of minutes. Add the lemon segments and stir through. Pour the jus into a jug or pitcher.

Serve the roast lamb on a platter along with the jus and Colcannon Mash (see page 158).

When cooking this recipe for rack of lamb, score the skin with the tip of a sharp knife in a lattice fashion, being careful not to pierce the flesh, before rubbing in the marinade.

SERVES 4

1 rack of lamb (with 10–12 bones)

FOR THE MARINADE
2 tbsp hoisin sauce
2 tsp grated fresh root ginger
2 tsp crushed peppercorns
2 tsp crushed garlic
1 tsp sesame seeds
1 tsp five-spice powder

Wexford Rack of Lamb with Asian Spices

Place all the marinade ingredients in a food processor and blitz until the mixture has a coarse consistency. Score the rack as described in the introduction and spread the mixture over it. Cover and marinate in the refrigerator for a least 1 hour before cooking, but preferably longer, if possible.

Preheat the oven to 190°C/375°F/gas mark 5. Cover the exposed bones in foil to prevent them from discolouring during cooking.

Place the lamb into a roasting pan and roast for 12–15 minutes for medium-rare. Set aside to rest for 15 minutes before serving.

Serve with some Potato Rösti (see page 160) and Caramelized Apple Chutney (see page 217).

I use cured air-dried lamb from McGeough's artisan butchers in Connemara. It is cured in local herbs, garlic, mint, lemon, orange and cloves for over 5 weeks, then dried and smoked, so it's packed full of flavour.

SERVES 4

3 garlic bulbs, cut in half horizontally
4 tbsp rapeseed (canola) oil
Salt and black pepper
250g (9oz) ready-made shortcrust
    pastry (pie dough)
Egg wash, made with 1 egg yolk, beaten

85g (3oz) Connemara air-dried lamb,
    thinly sliced (or use pancetta or
    bresaola)
1 tbsp chopped flat leaf parsley
200ml (1 cup) milk
2 egg yolks
50g (1 cup) fresh breadcrumbs

Connemara Air-dried Lamb and Garlic Tart

Preheat the oven to 200°C/400°F/gas mark 6.

Place the half-bulbs of garlic on a baking sheet lined with kitchen foil, drizzle with a little of the rapeseed oil and sprinkle with a pinch of salt, then seal tightly and roast for 30–35 minutes until the flesh is soft.

Reduce the oven temperature to 180°C/fan 160°C/gas mark 4. Roll out the pastry and use it to line a 20cm (8 inch) flan or tart tin. Chill in the refrigerator for 5 minutes.

Line the chilled pastry case with greaseproof paper or kitchen foil, lightly pressing it into the angles, then fill it with ceramic baking beans, dried pulses or rice. Bake for about 15 minutes. Remove the paper and beans, then bake the case for a further 5 minutes, or until it is dry and light golden brown. Brush the baked case immediately with egg wash, then return to the oven for 1 minute. Set aside while you make the filling.

Drizzle 2 tbsp of the rapeseed oil into a frying pan set over a medium heat. Quickly pan-fry the air-dried lamb for about 10–20 seconds. Add the parsley and set aside.

Mix together in a jug or small bowl the milk, egg yolks and breadcrumbs and season with salt and pepper.

Unwrap the roasted garlic bulb and squeeze the pulp into the pastry case. Spread it out evenly, then top with the lamb. Pour over the egg mixture and bake for 25 minutes. Serve warm.

Sweetbreads or *ris* are the culinary names for the thymus gland and pancreas of lamb. If you don't have any stock, use the liquid from poaching the sweetbread – just remember to use a lighter hand with the salt if you do.

SERVES 2

325g (11½oz) lamb sweetbreads
500ml (2 cups) light stock
Sea salt and black pepper
100g (⅔ cup) shelled broad (fava) beans
2 tbsp plain (all-purpose) flour
70g (5 tbsp) butter

1 shallot, finely diced
100g (3½oz) shiitake mushrooms, trimmed
1 tbsp vermouth
2 tbsp olive oil
200ml (1 cup) warm chicken stock or sweetbreads cooking liquid

Lamb Sweetbreads with Shiitake and Broad Beans

Soak the sweetbreads in several changes of cold water for a few hours. Drain and transfer them to a saucepan with the light stock and simmer for 3–4 minutes. Allow to cool, then trim off the sinews

Bring a small saucepan of water to the boil over a high heat. Add some sea salt and the broad beans and cook for about 2 minutes until just tender. Drain and refresh under cold running water. Now slip the outer skins off by pinching and squeezing. Place the beans in a small bowl of cold water and set aside. Discard the bitter skins.

Cut the sweetbreads into equal-sized pieces and season well with salt and black pepper. Next, coat them in the flour and shake off any excess. Set aside.

In a frying pan set over a medium heat, add 1 tbsp of the butter. When it is foaming, add the shallot and cook gently until soft. Add the mushrooms, increase the heat and cook them quickly until just tender. Add the vermouth and stir, then transfer the mixture to a bowl. Drain the broad beans and add them to the bowl.

Wipe out the pan, add the remaining butter with the olive oil and place the pan over a medium heat. When the fat is hot, add the sweetbreads, in batches if necessary, and cook for 8–10 minutes until they are golden and crispy on all sides. Transfer to a plate lined with kitchen paper (paper towels).

Tip out any fat in the pan and pour in the stock. Bring to the boil, then deglaze the pan, using a wooden spoon to scrape up the browned bits from the base of the pan. Boil for about 3 minutes until the liquid has reduced by half, then reduce the heat and add the mushroom mixture and sweetbreads to the pan. Cook gently until heated through and check the seasoning.

Divide the mixture between 4 serving plates and serve immediately.

There is nothing quite like the crackling off succulent roast pork. My tip for the crunchiest crackling is to score the skin in a criss-cross pattern, then rub it with some oil and rock salt.

SERVES 6–8

2kg (4½lb) rack of pork with skin attached, bottom bone removed but top bone left in
Sunflower oil
4 tsp rock (kosher) salt
Freshly ground black pepper
3–4 carrots, roughly sliced
2 onions, unpeeled, quartered

FOR THE APPLE COMPOTE
1–2 shallots, sliced
2 Granny Smith apples, peeled, cored and cut into small chunks
150ml (⅔ cup) apple cider
20g (1½ tbsp) butter
4 tbsp brown sugar
100g (⅔ cup) sultanas (golden raisins)
Rock salt and black pepper

Roast Pork with Crunchy Crackling

Preheat the oven to 180°C/fan 160°C/gas mark 4.

Score the fat on the pork in a criss-cross pattern with a very sharp knife. Drizzle with a little sunflower oil, rub with the rock salt and season with black pepper.

Place a large roasting pan over a high heat and drizzle in some oil. Sear the skin of the pork on all sides to seal. Remove from the heat, lay the carrots and onions in the bottom of the pan, then place the rack of pork on top.

Roast for 1¾–2 hours, allowing 30–35 minutes per 450g (1lb). At the end of the cooking time, the juices of the meat should run clear when the flesh is pierced with a metal skewer or the tip of a sharp knife, and the skin should be nice and crisp.

Meanwhile, to make the apple compote, take 2 tbsp cooking fat from the roasting pan and place it in a small saucepan. Add the shallots and cook over a medium heat for 2–3 minutes. Add the remaining ingredients and bring to the boil. Reduce the heat and cook for about 10 minutes until the compote has thickened.

When the pork is cooked, transfer it to a board, cover with kitchen foil and allow it to rest for 10–20 minutes until you are ready to eat.

Carve the meat and serve slices of pork and some crackling to everyone, with the apple compote alongside.

You might be forgiven for thinking that the sole difference between ham joints cooked on and off the bone is the presence of the bone itself. However, you will find that ham cooked on the bone has a superior taste and texture because the natural muscle, fat and bones are undisturbed. As it tends to come in bigger cuts, it will not suit everyone. Most people opt for the boneless option for ease of cooking and carving.

SERVES 10–12

1 whole fresh ham on the bone,
    about 7kg (15½lb)
About 4 tbsp cloves
3–4 tbsp homemade marmalade
    (such as the Orange Irish Whiskey
    Marmalade on page 211)
4 tbsp Irish whiskey
4 tbsp brown sugar

Whole Glazed Ham

Soak the ham in a bowl of water for up to 1 hour to remove any excess salt.

Place the ham in a large saucepan, cover with fresh water and bring to the boil. Reduce the heat and simmer for about 2½ hours. Turn off the heat and allow the meat to cool in the cooking liquid.

Preheat the oven to 150°C/300°F/gas mark 2.

Remove the ham from the cooking liquid, take off the outer rind and score a lattice pattern into the fat. Stud each diamond of fat with a clove, then put the ham into a roasting pan.

Put the marmalade and Irish whiskey into a saucepan set over a moderate heat and mix well until the marmalade has melted. Brush this mixture over the clove-studded ham, then sprinkle over the sugar.

Loosely cover the ham with kitchen foil and bake for about 1 hour or perhaps a little more (depending largely on your oven) until the fat has caramelized and is a golden brown colour. Remove the foil, increase the heat to 180°C/fan 160°C/gas mark 4 and cook for an additional 20 minutes.

Remove the ham from the oven and rest it for 30 minutes before slicing.

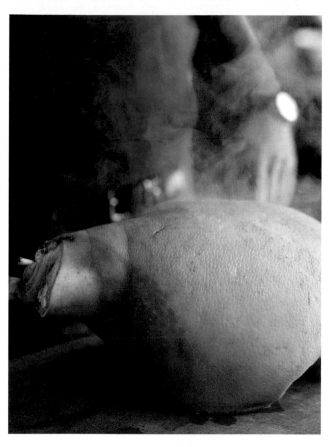

Pork belly is one of the tastiest cuts of meat. It can vary a lot in the actual amount of meat versus fat, so it helps to get to know your butcher and ask for a piece that's well layered with meat. This dish takes a little bit of preparation, as you cure the meat over the course of a couple of days, but it is worth it… a nice bit of slow-cooked pork belly is a melting piece of heaven.

SERVES 4–6

2 pieces of pork belly, about 1kg
  (2¼lb) each
4 tbsp salt
80g (⅓ cup) sugar
Grated rind of 3 lemons
1 tbsp finely chopped rosemary
Juice of 1 lemon

FOR THE BRINE
2 litres (8½ cups) water
150g (½ cup) salt
12–14 peppercorns
2–3 bay leaves
2 sprigs of thyme

FOR THE BALSAMIC GEL
250ml (1 cup) balsamic vinegar
⅓ tsp xanthan gum
125ml (½ cup) water

TO SERVE
40g (3 tbsp) butter
300g (2 cups) garden peas, blanched
300g (2 cups) broad (fava) beans,
  blanched
Salt and black pepper
200ml (1 cup) warm chicken stock

Lemon-cured Pork Belly with Balsamic Gel and Broad Beans

First make the brine (salt solution). Place all the ingredients into a large saucepan and bring to the boil, then reduce the heat and simmer for 30 minutes. Remove from the heat and allow the liquid to cool. Store the brine in the refrigerator until required.

Place the pork belly pieces in a dish and cover completely with the brine. Place in the refrigerator for 24 hours, then drain off the water and pat the pork belly dry.

Combine the salt and sugar in a small bowl and add the grated lemon rind and chopped rosemary. Rub the ingredients together with your fingers until fully incorporated and the mixture is fragrant. Add a squeeze of lemon juice. Place the pork belly into a clean dish, then rub the herb mixture into it. Cover the dish with clingfilm (plastic wrap) and place it in the refrigerator for about 24 hours.

When you are ready to cook, preheat the oven to 220°C/425°F/gas mark 7. Place the pork belly into a roasting pan and roast for 20 minutes, then reduce the heat to 180°C/350°F/gas mark 4 and roast for a further 30–40 minutes.

To make the balsamic gel, place the ingredients in a bowl and mix with a handheld blender until thickened. Set aside.

When the meat is ready, cook the vegetables. Melt the butter in a large sauté pan over a moderate heat. Add the peas and broad beans and season with salt. Add the chicken stock and let it reduce until it's all absorbed and the mixture is glazed.

Meanwhile, take the cooked pork belly out of the oven. You can either serve it as it is, cut into 4–6 portions, or slice it thinly and cook it in 1 tbsp melted pork fat or suet in a frying pan over a moderate heat for about 2–3 minutes on each side until caramelized.

Divide the vegetables equally between 4–6 warmed plates and top with the pork. Drizzle with the balsamic gel and sprinkle with salt and black pepper. Serve immediately.

It's best to use young and tender dandelion leaves for this refreshing salad, and harvest them before the flowers blossom or they will be bitter. If you find it difficult to get hold of dandelions, you can substitute chicory (endive).

SERVES 4

500g (1lb 2oz) young dandelion leaves
4 tsp vinegar
4 extremely fresh eggs
100g (3½oz) rashers (slices) of bacon
2 slices of white bread, diced
Flat leaf parsley, torn, to garnish

FOR THE DRESSING
4 tbsp oil
4 tsp vinegar
1 tsp Dijon mustard
Salt and black pepper

Dandelion Salad with Bacon and Poached Egg

Clean the dandelion leaves and wash them in several changes of water, checking for sand between the leaves. Dry them on kitchen paper (paper towels) or in a salad spinner and store them until required.

Bring a large saucepan of water to a simmer and add the vinegar. Fill a bowl with cold water and place it beside the cooker or stove. Poach the eggs in the water one at a time for about 3 minutes, then transfer them immediately to the cold water.

Place a frying pan on a medium-high heat and fry the bacon until crisp. Set aside. Add the cubes of bread to the empty pan and brown them for about 2 minutes on each side. Set aside.

Meanwhile, mix all the dressing ingredients in a small bowl.

Before serving, drizzle the dressing over the dandelion leaves and toss well. Divide the salad between 4 bowls or serving dishes, place the eggs, bacon and bread on top of the salad and garnish with parsley. Serve while still warm.

This warming, easy-to-make gratin is great for putting the Sunday lunch leftovers of bacon and potato to very good use. Serve it with dressed salad leaves or greens and a glass of white wine.

SERVES 4–6

1.25kg (2¾lb) firm potatoes
    (or 11 potatoes), left unpeeled and
    washed
1 tbsp rapeseed (canola) oil
200g (7oz) smoked bacon lardons
    (diced bacon)
1 onion, thinly sliced
4 garlic cloves, chopped
Salt and black pepper
300ml (1¼ cups) white wine
100ml (½ cup) double (heavy) cream
250g (9oz) Ardrahan cheese (or use a
    semi-soft cheese with a mature
    flavour), cut into large pieces

Ardrahan Cheese, Potato and Smoked Bacon Gratin

Place the potatoes in a large saucepan of cold water, bring to the boil and simmer for 20–30 minutes. You can monitor the cooking by pricking a potato with the tip of a knife. When they are cooked, the knife blade will slide into the potato without resistance. After cooking, drain and peel the potatoes.

Preheat the oven to 200°C/400°F/gas mark 6.

Meanwhile, drizzle the oil into a frying pan set over a medium-high heat. Add the smoked bacon and cook for a 2–5 minutes until golden brown. Add the onion, garlic and season with salt and black pepper and cook for a further 2–5 minutes. When the onion and garlic begin to take on colour, add the white wine to deglaze the pan, scraping up any bits from the base of the pan. Set aside.

Cut half the potatoes into thick slices and place them in the bottom of a gratin dish. Add half the bacon mixture. Cut the rest of the potatoes into strips and add them to the dish, followed by the remaining bacon mixture. Pour over the cream and place the pieces of Ardrahan cheese on top.

Bake until the cheese melts on the surface and enjoy the dish while it's hot.

White pudding is a versatile product that is normally part of a traditional Irish breakfast, but also works extremely well in this tart. The pork in the pudding and the caramelized apples are a wonderful taste combination. You can make the tarts with black pudding (blood sausage), if you like. Serve with some dressed salad leaves or greens.

SERVES 4

1 sheet of ready-rolled shortcrust pastry
    (pie dough), about 30 x 40cm
    (12 x 16 inches)
20g (1½ sticks) butter
3 apples, peeled, cored and diced
200g (7oz) Cashel Blue cheese (or use
    Gorgonzola cheese), diced
100g (3½oz) Ardrahan cheese (or use
    Brie cheese), cut into small slices
300g (10½oz) white pudding (or
    white boudin or other mild sausages),
    thinly sliced
Salt and black pepper

White Pudding, Cheese and Caramelized Apple Tarts

Preheat the oven to 180°C/350°F/gas mark 4.

Use the shortcrust pastry to line 4 individual pastry cases, each with a diameter of 10cm (4 inches). Chill for 10 minutes to avoid shrinkage while baking, then blind bake (see page 112) for 15 minutes. Remove the paper and beans, then bake the case for a further 5 minutes, or until it is dry and light golden brown. Brush the baked case immediately with egg wash, then return to the oven for 1 minute. Set aside while you make the filling.

In a frying pan set over a medium heat, melt the butter and add the apples. Cook for 5 minutes, until the pieces are lightly caramelized but still slightly firm.

Fill the baked pastry cases (shells) with the cheeses and apples, then layer the thin slices of white pudding on the top.

Bake for about 5 minutes, until the tarts are crispy. Serve immediately.

HERB GARDEN

Vegetarian

This delicious risotto is made using orzo, a rice-shaped pasta, instead of rice. The flavour of Cratloe sheep's cheese, a local product, really enhances the dish, but you could substitute Parmesan if you like.

SERVES 4

50g (2 tbsp) butter
2 shallots, finely diced
2 sprigs of thyme, torn
Salt and black pepper
400g (14oz) orzo pasta
250ml (1 cup) dry white wine
700ml (3 cups) warm vegetable stock
  or water

4 tbsp olive oil
16 asparagus spears, trimmed (if the
  spears are thick, cut them in half
  lengthways)
3 sprigs of oregano
Grated rind and juice of 1 lemon
70g (2½oz) Cratloe sheep's cheese or
  Parmesan cheese, grated, plus extra
  shavings to serve

Asparagus, Cratloe Sheep's Cheese and Orzo Risotto

Place a wide, heavy-based saucepan over a low heat and slowly melt the butter. Add the chopped shallots, thyme and seasoning and cook very gently until the shallot is completely softened.

Add the orzo pasta and mix well to ensure it does not stick to the bottom of the pan. Allow it to become glazed and cook without any liquid for 1 minute while stirring constantly.

Next, add the white wine and continue to stir the pasta. The wine will evaporate quite quickly, so you really need to stand over this dish as you cook it.

Increase the heat slightly and start adding the stock little by little, never adding a ladleful until the previous one has evaporated. It is vitally important not to rush this process. Continue in this way until you have added all of the liquid and the pasta is plump and tender.

In the meantime, heat the oil in a large frying pan over a high heat. Add the asparagus and stir-fry for 2–3 minutes, then stir in the oregano and lemon rind. Switch off the heat and fold in the pasta.

To obtain a nice creamy risotto, stir in the cheese, check the seasoning and finish with the lemon juice. Serve immediately, with additional cheese.

This is a lovely light vegetarian dish with ribbons of blanched courgette and a light lemon and olive oil dressing.

SERVES 4

Salt and black pepper
4 courgettes (zucchini), sliced into
     ribbons with a mandoline or potato
     peeler
2 tbsp olive oil
3 garlic cloves, chopped
2 tbsp sesame seeds
Grated rind and juice of 1 lemon

Courgette Tagliatelli

Bring a large saucepan of salted water to the boil. Place a bowl of ice-cold water on the side.

Blanch the courgette ribbons in batches in the boiling water for 1–2 minutes. Remove them with a slotted spoon and place immediately in the cold water for 2 minutes. Drain well.

Heat a large frying pan with half the olive oil. Add the courgette ribbons and fry for 1–2 minutes, then add the garlic, sesame seeds, lemon rind and seasoning and toss the mixture to combine. Do not overdo it – you want to avoid breaking up the ribbons.

Remove from the heat and drizzle with the remaining olive oil and the lemon juice. Serve immediately.

Here's a curry that makes a substantial main course but can also be served as a lovely side dish. Add a bit more chilli if you like it hot.

SERVES 4

3 tsp olive oil
2 onions, finely sliced
1 tsp cumin seeds
2 tsp grated fresh root ginger
3 garlic cloves, finely chopped
1–2 hot green chillies, deseeded and finely chopped
2 tsp turmeric
1 tbsp garam masala
2 tsp ground coriander
1 tsp ground cumin
300g (10½oz) potatoes (about 2–3 potatoes), cut into small pieces
300ml (1¼ cups) vegetable stock
2 tomatoes, chopped
1 cauliflower, cut into florets
150g (1 cup) fresh or frozen peas
2 tbsp chopped fresh coriander (cilantro), chopped
Natural (plain) yogurt, to serve (optional)

Cauliflower, Pea and Potato Curry

Heat the oil in a large wok or deep nonstick saucepan. Add the onions and cumin seeds and cook until the onion has softened. Add the ginger, garlic and chillies and cook for 2–3 minutes until aromatic. Add the remaining spices to the pan and stir well.

Next, add the potatoes and stir until coated in the spices. Sauté for 3–4 minutes, then reduce the heat, pour in the stock and chopped tomatoes and cook for 10–15 minutes until the potato has softened.

Mix in the cauliflower, cover the pan and cook for 10 minutes. Next, stir in the peas and cook for a further 10 minutes until all the vegetables are cooked through. Remove from the heat and add the coriander.

Serve the curry with steamed basmati or other long-grain rice and drizzle with some natural yogurt, if liked.

Here's my savoury take on the French classic. As the tomatoes cook in the caramel, they become sweet and tender. Served with some fresh green leaves, this dish makes a perfect starter or light lunch.

SERVES 4

2 tbsp honey
800g (1¾lb) cherry tomatoes
Salt and black pepper
1 sheet of ready-rolled puff pastry, about
   35 x 23cm (14 x 9 inches)
Egg wash, made with 1 egg yolk, beaten
50g (⅔ cup) Parmesan cheese shavings
200g (7 cups) mixture of basil and
   rocket (arugula) leaves
20ml (4 tsp) olive oil

Cherry Tomato Tarte Tatin

Preheat the oven to 200°C/400°F/gas mark 6.

Combine the honey and cherry tomatoes in a 23cm (9-inch) ovenproof frying pan. Spread the tomatoes evenly across the pan and season with salt and black pepper.

Cut a 23cm (9-inch) circle from the puff pastry and place it over the pan. Brush with egg wash, then bake in the oven for 20–25 minutes. Set aside to rest for 5–8 minutes so that the tomatoes reabsorb their juices.

Place a large serving platter over the pan and invert both to reveal a glorious pastry case laden with caramelized cherry tomatoes. Add some Parmesan shavings and a few basil and rocket leaves. Serve on a bed of the remaining basil and rocket leaves, lightly dressed in olive oil.

In Greece, where it originated, this pie is known as *spanakopita*. Boilie goats' cheese is soft with a very light taste.

SERVES 4

4 tbsp olive oil
1 red onion, finely chopped
4 spring onions (scallions), sliced
200g (3 cups) mushrooms, chopped
1 leek, trimmed and thinly sliced
1kg (2¼lb) spinach, tough stems removed
1 small bunch of oregano

350g (12oz) Boilie goats' cheese, crumbled
Salt and black pepper
3 eggs, beaten
500g (1lb 2oz) ready-rolled filo (phyllo) pastry
200g (7oz) butter, melted

Spinach and Goats' Cheese Filo Pastry Pie

Heat the olive oil in a large frying pan and sauté the red onion, spring onions, mushrooms and leek for 2–3 minutes until translucent. Add the spinach and sauté for 5–8 minutes until the leaves have wilted and the liquid has cooked off.

Remove the pan from the heat and allow the contents to cool. When cool enough to handle, finely chop the spinach mixture and place it in a large bowl.

Preheat the oven to 180°C/350°F/gas mark 4. Lightly oil a round metal cake tin with a diameter of 30cm (12 inches) or a 25 x 38cm (10 x 15-inch) rectangular baking dish.

Add the oregano and goats' cheese to the spinach. Season with salt and black pepper to taste. Pour the eggs over the mixture and give it a stir to combine the ingredients well.

Open up the filo pastry and place it on a work surface. Cover with a damp cloth.

Taking 1 filo sheet at a time, brush it with melted butter and use to line the cake tin or baking dish, allowing it to overhang the sides. Repeat this step, using half the sheets.

Using a wooden spoon, spread half the spinach mixture over the layered pastry. Cover with 2 more sheets of buttered pastry, then spread the remaining spinach over them. Fold in the overhanging pastry, then butter and layer the remaining pastry sheets on top. Using a sharp knife, score portion shapes into the upper layers of pastry.

Bake the pie for about 40–45 minutes, moving it to the bottom shelf for the last 15–20 minutes, until golden brown and crisp.

Traditionally, if you couldn't afford lamb or even stewing beef, you'd cook 'blind stew', so called because it has no meat you can see. Nowadays, it is considered a very tasty vegetarian dish. A bit of crusty bread is the perfect accompaniment to this one-pot wonder dinner.

SERVES 6–8

1 tbsp olive oil
350g (12oz) shallots
2 leeks, trimmed and thickly sliced
½ swede (rutabaga), chopped into chunks
2 parsnips, quartered
350g (12oz) carrots (about 6 carrots), sliced
175g (6oz) pearl barley
225ml (1 cup) white wine
1 litre (4¼ cups) vegetable stock
1 bay leaf
3 sprigs of thyme
Small bunch of parsley, finely chopped
Salt and black pepper

FOR THE DUMPLINGS
100g (¾ cup) self-raising flour
    (or ¾ cup all-purpose flour + ¾ tsp baking powder)
50g (4 tbsp) unsalted butter
50g (½ cup) Wexford or good mature/sharp Cheddar cheese, grated
2 tsp finely chopped flat leaf parsley
2 tbsp water

Blind Irish Stew

Heat the oil in a large flameproof casserole dish over a moderate heat. Add the shallots and cook for 5–6 minutes until they start to soften and brown. Add the leeks and cook for 2 minutes, then stir in the swede, parsnips and carrots. Pour in the barley and wine and cook until the liquid has reduced by half.

Add the stock, bay leaf, thyme and parsley and season with salt and black pepper. Cover the pan with a lid, bring to the boil, then reduce the heat and simmer for 45 minutes, stirring occasionally, until the barley and vegetables are tender.

Meanwhile, heat the oven to 200°C/400°F/gas mark 6 and make the dumplings. Rub the flour and butter together until the mixture resembles breadcrumbs. Add the cheese and parsley and mix well. Sprinkle over the water and mix to form a soft dough. Divide the dough into 6 equal parts and roll each of these into a ball. Dot these on top of the stew.

Transfer the casserole to the oven and cook, uncovered, for 20–25 minutes until the dumplings are golden.

I like to use Rooster potatoes as they are grown locally, but a good alternative would be Maris Piper or Yukon Gold, great all-rounders with a fluffy, creamy texture when cooked. You could add some Cheddar for an even richer pie.

SERVES 4

500g (1lb 2oz) potatoes (about
    2 potatoes), very thinly sliced
2 garlic cloves, finely chopped
2 tbsp chopped flat leaf parsley
Salt and black pepper
200ml (1 cup) pouring (light) cream
Flour, for dusting
400g (14oz) ready-made puff pastry
Egg wash, made with 1 egg yolk beaten
    with 1 tsp milk

Puff Pastry Potato Pie

Preheat the oven to 190°C/375°C/gas mark 5.

Put the potatoes, garlic, parsley and some salt and pepper into a saucepan and pour in the cream. Cook over a moderate heat for about 10 minutes until the potato has softened slightly.

On a lightly floured work surface, roll out the pastry and cut out a circle about 8cm (3 inches) wider than the top of your pie dish. Using a sharp knife, lightly score the pastry in a lattice pattern, ensuring you don't cut right through it.

Pour the potato mixture into your pie dish. Brush the egg wash over the top and around the edges of the dish, then cover with the pastry. Press to secure it, then brush with more egg wash.

Bake for about 15 minutes until the pastry is light and golden.

This easy-to-make dish is perfect for a lunch or quick supper. I love the flavour of the lovely organic St Tola goats' cheese, but you can use whatever goats' cheeses are local to you. Some toasted slices of French stick or bread would make a great addition.

SERVES 4

400g (14oz) spinach, thick stalks
   trimmed
25g (2 tbsp) softened butter, plus extra
   for greasing
Salt and black pepper
100g (3½oz) St Tola goats' cheese
4 tbsp pouring (light) cream
4 eggs

Baked Eggs with Spinach

Preheat the oven to 190°C/375°F/gas mark 5.

Put the spinach into a large saucepan, add 2 tbsp water, cover with a lid and cook for about 2–3 minutes until the spinach is wilted.

Drain well, pressing out all the excess water, then return it to the pan with about a quarter of the butter, stirring until the spinach is glistening.

Butter 4 ramekins, then sprinkle some salt and black pepper into them.

Divide the spinach between the ramekins, then add the goats' cheese and cream. Break an egg into each dish, top with a slice of butter. Bake for 10–15 minutes, until the eggs are just set. Serve immediately.

Salads and Side Dishes

If you like, you could substitute sweet potatoes for the baby potatoes. Feta or goats' cheese can make a wonderful addition to this salad too.

SERVES 6

500g (1lb 2oz) baby potatoes
2 beetroot (beets), unpeeled
3 tbsp olive oil
Salt and black pepper
Juice of 1 lemon
2 spring onions (scallions), chopped
2 radishes, very thinly sliced
1 red onion, very thinly sliced
100g (3 cups) watercress leaves
50g (1 cup) flat leaf parsley, stems
    discarded

Beetroot and Baby Potato Salad

Preheat the oven to 180°C/350°F/gas mark 4.

Boil the potatoes in a saucepan of salted water for about 15 minutes, until soft to the point of a knife. Strain and set aside to cool, then remove the skins.

Wash the beetroot, then wrap in kitchen foil with a little drizzle of olive oil and some salt and black pepper. Place the foil parcel in a roasting pan and bake for 1–1½ hours until the beetroot has softened. Allow to cool, then remove the skin.

Cut the beetroot into 2cm (¾-inch) cubes and place in a serving bowl. Drizzle with some of the olive oil and lemon juice.

Cut the potatoes into cubes and add to the beetroot together with the spring onions, radishes, red onion, watercress leaves and parsley. Drizzle with the remaining olive oil and lemon juice. Season before serving.

On Irish shores, samphire seaweed is found in abundance. Pick only the top few inches of the little plants because these are the most tender. To store your seaweed, keep it in a damp cloth inside a freezer bag. To retain its crunch and salty kick, it needs just a few minutes of cooking.

SERVES 4–6

300g (10½oz) samphire (also known
    as sea asparagus or salicornia)
1 tsp balsamic vinegar
Grated rind and juice of 1 lemon
2 tsp extra virgin olive oil
Pinch of oregano
Coarse sea salt and black pepper

Samphire Salad

Bring a large saucepan of water to the boil and blanch the samphire for 30 seconds. Transfer immediately to a bowl of iced water, then drain well.

Place the remaining ingredients in a bowl and mix together. Add the samphire and toss to coat in the dressing. Serve warm or cold

Simple Rocket Salad

We have a very extensive selection of lettuces in our garden at Dunbrody, but rocket is one of my favourite salad greens. Often we make a light lunch out of just these leaves, dressing them very simply and accompanying them with nothing more than a large chunk of crusty bread.

SERVES 4

300g (10½oz) rocket (arugula) leaves
50g (1¾oz) Parmesan cheese (optional)
50g (1⅔ cups) croutons (optional)
Juice of 1 lemon
2 tbsp olive oil
Salt and black pepper

Arrange the leaves in a large serving bowl or on a platter.

With a vegetable peeler, shave slices of Parmesan, if using, over the leaves. Scatter the croutons on top, if using.

Mix the lemon juice and olive oil together in a bowl and season lightly.

Just as you are ready to eat the salad, dress the leaves with the tangy dressing and serve immediately.

Celeriac Waldorf Salad

A beautiful combination of sweet, savoury and crunchy, this salad was inspired by the famous Waldorf Astoria Hotel in New York. There are many different variations, but sometimes the simplest is best, so this is my favourite.

SERVES 4

100g (1 cup) dry-roasted walnuts
2 green apples, peeled, cored and cut into matchsticks
1 head of celeriac, peeled and cut into matchsticks
2 celery sticks, cut into matchsticks

FOR THE DRESSING
4 tbsp crème fraîche
1 tsp Dijon mustard
4 tbsp extra virgin olive oil
1 tbsp lemon juice
Salt and black pepper

Whisk the dressing ingredients in a large bowl until combined.

Just before serving, add the salad ingredients and gently stir to coat.

This is a lovely crunchy and tangy accompaniment to cold meats and salads. Store any leftovers in the refrigerator and use within a few days.

MAKES ABOUT 750G (1LB 10OZ)

500g (1lb 2oz) red cabbage (or
   1 small head), core removed
   and leaves thinly sliced
1 onion, thinly sliced
50g (⅓ cup) sultanas
   (golden raisins)
2 tbsp white wine vinegar
2 tbsp muscovado sugar
   or light brown sugar
250g (9oz) cooking apples (or 2 cooking
   apples), peeled, cored and sliced

15g (1 tbsp) butter
½ tsp ground mixed spice (allspice)
1 tsp salt
Freshly ground black pepper
Grated rind and juice of 1 orange

Pickled Sweet and Sour Red Cabbage

Preheat the oven to 150°C/300°F/gas mark 2.

Layer the cabbage, onion, sultanas, vinegar, sugar, apples, butter and mixed spice into a baking dish and season with the salt and some black pepper. Add the orange rind and juice.

Cover the dish with kitchen foil and bake for 2½ hours, removing the foil for the last 20 minutes of cooking. Serve hot or cold.

These mushrooms are wonderful served hot with meats or as a base for fish. They are also good cold – as a condiment, a component of a salad, or even as the main ingredient, garnished with similarly preserved tomatoes and shaved radishes. Use a variety of mushrooms for textural and taste contrast.

MAKES ABOUT 1.5KG (3LB 5OZ)

1kg (2¼lb) forest mushrooms, such as
    shiitakes, morels, chanterelles,
    porcini, cep, trumpet and oyster
    mushrooms
400ml (1¾ cups) extra virgin olive
    oil, plus extra to top up the jar if
    necessary
2 bay leaves
4 sprigs of thyme
2 sprigs of rosemary
1 tsp smoked paprika
3 tbsp sherry vinegar
Salt and black pepper

Pickled Forest Mushrooms

Remove the shiitake stems, along with any other stems that are tough, and discard them or set them aside for another use (such as in a vegetable stock). Trim any remaining stems any cut out any bruised areas. Tear larger mushrooms into bite-sized pieces (bear in mind that they will shrink as they cook) and leave small mushrooms whole. Score the large mushrooms so that they will absorb the pickling juices.

Pour the oil into a large wide saucepan, then add the bay leaves, thyme and rosemary. Stir in the smoked paprika and heat the oil until it reaches 75°C (167°F).

Add the mushrooms to the pan and toss to coat in the oil. Cook for 5 minutes, gently turning from time to time. The mushrooms will gradually submerge in the oil as they cook and wilt.

Remove the pan from the heat, then stir in the vinegar and season with salt and black pepper. Leave the mushrooms to steep for at least 1 hour. Transfer the mushrooms and aromatic oil into sterilized containers (see page 209) and, if necessary, pour in more olive oil to cover the mushrooms. Seal tightly, then label and date. Keep refrigerated and use within 1 month. Remove from the refrigerator at least 1 hour before serving to bring back to room temperature.

Sweet and Sour Carrots

These tasty carrots are vibrant, crunchy and complement almost any main dish. Be careful not to overcook them or they will lose their vivid colour.

SERVES 6

500g (1lb 2oz) carrots (preferably baby carrots)
50g (4 tbsp) butter
4 tbsp caster (superfine) sugar
100ml (½ cup) white wine vinegar
1 sprig of rosemary
4 tbsp water
Salt and black pepper

Place the carrots in a small sauté pan over a medium heat. Add the butter, sugar, white wine vinegar and rosemary and allow to simmer for 5–10 minutes. Pour in the water and cook the carrots until tender. Season with salt and black pepper.

Roasted Butternut Squash Mousseline

Butternut squash is a comforting autumnal vegetable that is packed with vitamins and fibre. Always buy ones without blemishes and do not store them in the refrigerator.

SERVES 4

2 butternut squash, halved lengthways and deseeded
4 garlic cloves
4 sprigs of thyme
Salt and black pepper
Olive oil
100g (1 stick) butter

Place the butternut squash halves cut-side up on a baking sheet and put a garlic clove and sprig of thyme in each ones. Season with salt and black pepper, then drizzle with a little olive oil and transfer to the oven. Bake for 35–45 minutes, until the squash is cooked through and golden. Cover with kitchen foil during cooking if necessary to avoid burning it.

Once cooked, scoop out the squash pulp from the skin and place in a food processor with the garlic. Add the butter and some more seasoning and blitz until puréed.

This is a fantastic way of cooking Brussels sprouts and it makes for a very interesting vegetable option.

SERVES 6

500g (1lb 2oz) Brussels sprouts, trimmed and rough outer leaves removed
Salt and black pepper
25g (2 tbsp) butter
115g (1 cup) chestnuts
1 tbsp brown sugar
70g (¾ cup) cranberries

Brussels Sprouts with Chestnuts and Cranberries

Using a sharp knife, cut a cross into the bottom of each Brussels sprout.

Bring a saucepan of salted water to the boil, add the sprouts and boil for 6–8 minutes until they are soft and tender. Drain off the water.

Meanwhile, in a large saucepan or wok, melt the butter and quickly fry the chestnuts until they are starting to colour. Add the sugar and cranberries and continue to cook until the sugar has dissolved and the chestnuts are slightly caramelized.

Add the sprouts and toss around in the pan, ensuring they are well combined and piping hot. Season with salt and pepper and serve immediately.

Chestnut, Cranberry and Sausagemeat Stuffing

This traditional recipe makes a wonderful stuffing for turkey or goose. Fresh cranberries are readily available in Ireland during the winter, so are frequently used in Christmas dishes.

MAKES ABOUT 500G (1LB 2OZ)

225g (8oz) sausagement
150g (3 cups) fresh white breadcrumbs
1 tbsp chopped flat leaf parsley
1 tbsp chopped thyme
1 tsp black pepper
2 onions, finely diced
50g (½ cup) chestnuts, chopped
50g (½ cup) fresh or frozen cranberries
2 garlic cloves, crushed

Preheat the oven to 180°C/350°F/gas mark 4.

In a large bowl, mix together the sausagemeat, breadcrumbs, chopped herbs and black pepper.

Add the onions, chestnuts, cranberries and garlic and mix all the ingredients together.

Place the stuffing in the cavity of a turkey (see page 80) and cook as instructed, or place the mixture in a roasting pan, cover with kitchen foil and cook for 25–30 minutes.

Sage and Onion Stuffing

Try adding cranberries to this stuffing before placing it in the oven. It can be served as a side dish if you prefer not to stuff your turkey.

MAKES ABOUT 450G (1LB)

150g (1½ sticks) butter
1 large onion, finely chopped
250g (5 cups) fresh white breadcrumbs
1 tbsp chopped sage
1 tbsp chopped thyme
4 tbsp chopped flat leaf parsley
Salt and black pepper

Preheat the oven to 180°C/350°F/gas mark 4.

Melt the butter in a large frying pan over a medium heat. Add the onion and sauté for 3–4 minutes until it is softened and translucent, but not coloured.

Put the breadcrumbs and herbs into a large ovenproof dish. Mix well and season to taste.

Pour the butter and onion mixture over the breadcrumb and herb mixture, then bake for 20–25 minutes until golden. Remove the stuffing from the oven and serve immediately.

If using this stuffing for turkey (see page 80), please ensure it has cooled down before you stuff it into the body cavity.

I use some lovely smoked Gubbeen cheese in this dish, but a good-quality blue cheese, such as Cashel Blue, can work just as well.

SERVES 4

1kg (2lb 4oz) baby leeks
25g (2 tbsp) butter
2½ tbsp plain (all-purpose) flour
300ml (1¼ cups) milk
100g (3½oz) smoked Gubbeen cheese
    (or use a semi-soft cows' cheese)
Salt and black pepper

Baby Leek Gratin with Smoked Gubbeen

Preheat the oven to 200°C/400°F/gas mark 6.

Bring a large saucepan of salted water to the boil. Add the leeks and blanch for 3–6 minutes until tender. Remove them with a slotted spoon, drain thoroughly and place in an ovenproof dish. Reserve 200ml (1 cup) of the leek cooking water.

Meanwhile, melt the butter in a saucepan over a medium heat and stir in the flour. Cook for about 2 minutes until a light golden colour. Pour in the milk and reserved water and whisk vigorously until smooth.

Bring to a simmer and cook for 8–10 minutes. Remove from the heat and add the cheese, stirring until melted.

Pour the sauce over the leeks and season with salt and black pepper. Place the dish in the oven and bake for 5 minutes until caramelized.

As they have a mild taste, courgettes need a little flavour boost during cooking, be it with the addition of garlic, rosemary or thyme. Courgettes can be steamed, fried or sautéed, but I don't recommend boiling them because they don't retain their flavour.

SERVES 4

5 courgettes (zucchini), cut into slices
    2cm (¾-inch) thick
Salt and black pepper
4–5 tbsp olive oil
2 onions, thinly sliced
3 garlic cloves, chopped
70g (¾ cup) Parmesan cheese, grated
3 eggs
150ml (⅔ cup) double (heavy) cream
100ml (½ cup) milk
3 sprigs of oregano

Courgette Gratin

Place the courgette slices into a colander and sprinkle with salt. Leave for 1 hour to release some of their water, then rinse and leave to drain, or place them on a large towel to dry.

Preheat the oven to 200°C/400°F/gas mark 6.

Heat 1 tbsp of the olive oil in a large saucepan over a high heat. Add the onions and garlic and season with salt and black pepper. Cook for 3–4 minutes until the onion is caramelized. Transfer to a side dish and place the empty pan back over a high heat.

Add 1 more tbsp olive oil and cook the courgettes in batches for 1–2 minutes to caramelize.

Drizzle 2 tbsp olive oil into the bottom of an ovenproof dish and sprinkle over a little of the grated Parmesan. Arrange a layer of the caramelized courgettes on top, followed by a layer of the onion and garlic mixture. Continue making layers, finishing with a layer of the courgettes.

In a bowl, combine the eggs with the cream, milk, oregano and some salt and black pepper. Pour the mixture into the baking dish, sprinkle over the rest of the Parmesan and bake for 20 minutes. Serve immediately.

Champ, a delicious mixture of creamy potato and onions, should
be soft in consistency but not sloppy. Once mastered, this recipe
can be adapted for different results. Try replacing the milk with
crème fraîche or Quark (skimmed-milk soft cheese), or add some
steamed cabbage to turn it into that other Irish favourite, Colcannon
(see page 158).

SERVES 4–6

675g (1lb 8oz) potatoes (or 6 potatoes),
    left unpeeld and scrubbed
Salt and white pepper
6 tbsp milk
4 spring onions (scallions),
    finely chopped
50g (4 tbsp) butter

Champ

Cover the potatoes with cold water in a saucepan and add a pinch of salt. Bring
to the boil, then simmer for 15–20 minutes or until completely tender when pierced
with the tip of a sharp knife.

Heat the milk in a saucepan with the spring onions for 5 minutes until the onions
have softened.

Drain the potatoes in a colander, then peel them while they are still hot. Push
through a potato ricer, or through a sieve or strainer using a palette knife or spatula.

Beat 40g (3 tbsp) of the butter into the warm mashed potato, then mix in the milk
and spring onion mixture. Season with salt and white pepper to taste.

To serve, spoon the champ into a warmed serving dish and make a slight dip in the
middle. Add the remaining butter and allow it to melt in.

This is a classic Irish dish that brings together Ireland's two favourite vegetables – potatoes and cabbage. I love eating this all year round and have been known to eat a large bowl with just a knob or pat of butter and a big spoon.

SERVES 4

550g (1lb 4oz) potatoes (or 5 potatoes),
    unpeeled
50g (4 tbsp) butter
Salt and black pepper
4 tbsp double (heavy) cream
50g (1¾oz) back bacon, finely chopped
50g (¾ cup) green cabbage,
    finely chopped

Colcannon Mash

Cover the potatoes with cold water in a saucepan and add a pinch of salt. Bring to the boil, then simmer for 15–20 minutes or until the flesh is tender when pierced with the point of a knife. Drain in a colander, then peel them while they are still hot. Mash the potato until smooth. Add 40g (3 tbsp) of the butter and season with salt and black pepper to taste.

Meanwhile, heat the cream in a saucepan. Just as it comes to the boil, pour it into the mashed potato and beat well.

Fry the bacon and cabbage in a saucepan with the remaining butter for 5 minutes until softened. Add to the potato and mix well. Keep warm until ready to serve.

Chive Mash

This is a very simple way of jazzing up a simple commodity such as mashed potato. You could substitute spring onions (scallions), wholegrain mustard or even some freshly grated horseradish for the chives.

SERVES 4

500g (1lb 2oz) potatoes (or 4 potatoes), cut into chunks
4 tbsp double (heavy) cream
25g (2 tbsp) butter
Salt and black pepper
4 tbsp snipped chives

Cover the potatoes with cold water in a saucepan, add a pinch of salt and bring to the boil. Cook for 15–20 minutes until soft to the point of a knife, then strain.

In a small saucepan, heat the cream gently and add the butter, then pour over the potatoes. Mash the potatoes and season with a little salt and black pepper. Add the chives and incorporate thoroughly with a wooden spoon. Serve immediately.

Pancetta and Cheese Mash

The recipe for this buttery, cheesy mash can be adapted for different results. For sheer indulgence, add a tablespoon or two of cream for a richer mash.

SERVES 6

1kg (2lb 4oz) Rooster, Yukon Gold or similar potatoes (or 9 potatoes), unpeeled and scrubbed
Salt and black pepper
6 slices of pancetta
85g (6 tbsp) butter
200g (1¾ cups) smoked Cheddar cheese, grated

Cover the potatoes with cold water in a saucepan and add a pinch of salt. Bring to the boil, then simmer for 15–20 minutes or until completely tender when pierced with the tip of a sharp knife.

Meanwhile, crisp the pancetta slices under the grill or broiler, then, when slightly cooled, break them into shards.

Drain the potatoes in a colander, then peel them while they are still hot. Push them through a potato ricer, or through a sieve or strainer using a palette knife or spatula. Beat half the butter into the mash, then add the smoked Cheddar and mix well. Season with salt and black pepper to taste.

To serve, spoon the potatoes into a warmed serving dish and make a slight dip in the middle. Add the remaining butter and allow it to melt in.

Sprinkle the crushed pancetta over the mash, then serve immediately.

Potato Rösti

All you need for a decent rösti are firm potatoes, butter, seasoning and some oil to cook it in the pan until the edges are crisp and golden. If I'm feeling indulgent, I use duck or goose fat.

SERVES 4

3–4 large potatoes, grated
Salt and black pepper
50g (4 tbsp) butter
4–5 tbsp sunflower or rapeseed (canola) oil

Preheat the oven to 140°C/275°F/gas mark 1.

Place the grated potato on a clean tea or dish towel and squeeze out the liquid by twisting the towel. Place the potato in a bowl and season with some salt and black pepper.

Melt the butter and oil in a large frying pan set over a moderate heat. Take small handfuls of the grated potato and make little patties with a diameter of 5–6cm (2–2½ inches). Place them in the pan and fry for about 5–6 minutes on each side. When cooked, they should be crisp and dry.

Place the cooked rösti on a greased baking sheet in the oven to keep warm. Repeat this process until all the potato has been used.

Sauteéd Garlic Potatoes

This is a wonderful alternative to chips or fries, and so much simpler to prepare. Use beef dripping or oil instead of duck fat for different flavours.

SERVES 4

5 potatoes, cut into slices 2–3mm (¹⁄₁₆–¹⁄₈ inch) thick
100g (½ cup) duck fat
Salt and black pepper
3 garlic cloves, crushed
2 tbsp chopped flat leaf parsley

Wash the potato slices and pat them dry on kitchen paper (paper towels).

Heat a tablespoon of the duck fat in a saucepan. Add the potatoes and cook over a moderate heat for 15–20 minutes, stirring to brown all sides. Season with salt and black pepper.

Mix the garlic and parsley in a bowl, then add to the potatoes. Cover the pan and cook for another 3–5 minutes, and season once again, if necessary.

Dauphinoise Potatoes

This classic potato dish needs long, slow cooking to ensure soft slices of garlic-flavoured potato. Don't scrimp on the cream otherwise the top layer will dry out. Use a mandoline to cut the potatoes into thin slices of uniform thickness. If they are cut too thickly, the cream will evaporate before the potatoes are cooked. For a version of this dish to serve with roast beef, add 2 teaspoons of grated horseradish along with the garlic.

SERVES 4–6

7–8 large potatoes, thinly sliced
1 onion, finely sliced
2 garlic cloves, finely chopped
70g (5 tbsp) butter
Salt and black pepper
100g (1 cup) grated Cheddar cheese or
    mozzarella (optional)
500ml (2 cups) double (heavy) cream

Preheat the oven to 160°C/325°F/gas mark 3.

Layer the potatoes, onion and garlic in individual dishes or a large casserole dish, sprinkling butter, seasoning and cheese on each layer.

Pour the cream into a saucepan and bring to the boil, then pour it over the potatoes until they are almost covered. Depending on the size of your dish(es), you may need more or less cream than listed above.

Cover with kitchen foil and bake for up to 1 hour. Serve immediately.

Boulangère Potatoes

The sweet onion adds delicious flavour to the potato, which can be served with any roasted meat dish. I always serve my Roast Leg of Lamb with a Red Wine Reduction (see page 106) on a bed of these potatoes.

SERVES 4–6

900g (2lb) Roosters, Maris Piper, Yukon Gold or
    similar potatoes (or 8 potatoes), uniformly sliced
2 large onions, thinly sliced
Salt and black pepper
200ml (1 cup) warm chicken or vegetable stock

Preheat the oven to 220°C/425°F/gas mark 7.

Place a layer of potatoes in an ovenproof dish, then add a layer of the onions and season with salt and black pepper. Continue layering in this way, finishing with a layer of potato.

Pour in the stock, then place the dish on the lowest rack of the oven and cook for 1½–1¾ hours.

Potato cakes made with mashed potatoes and bound with flour and egg yolks are a traditional accompaniment to Irish meals. Here they are flavoured with dulse seaweed before being breaded and shallow-fried.

SERVES 4

700g (1lb 9oz) potatoes (or 6 potatoes), cut into pieces
200g (1¾ sticks) butter
400g (8 cups) fresh breadcrumbs
40g (⅓ cup) plain (all-purpose) flour
20g (¾oz) dulse or other seaweed, such as arame, hijiki or wakame, finely chopped

Salt and black pepper
2 egg yolks
Olive oil, for frying

Dulse Potatoes

Cover the potatoes with cold water in a saucepan, add a pinch of salt and bring to the boil. Simmer for 30–40 minutes until softened. Remove from the heat and pass the potato through a potato ricer.

In the meantime, melt the butter in a saucepan and, when foaming, add the breadcrumbs and fry for 3–4 minutes until golden. Transfer to a plate and set aside until cooled.

Mash the potatoes in a large bowl, then add the flour and dulse. Season with salt and black pepper to taste, then combine thoroughly. Mix in the egg yolks, then divide the potato into 12–15 patties. Roll these in the breadcrumbs and pat to coat evenly.

Heat some olive oil in a frying pan set over a medium heat. Add the potato patties and cook for about 4 minutes on each side or until golden and hot in the centre.

This is my mum's recipe and it has never failed me. There's no doubt that the fat from roasting meat makes the best roast potatoes. Alternatively, if you ever roast a goose or duck, save every drop of the fat and freeze it in ice cube trays, then bag it to use at your leisure – even a couple added to your oil will help the flavour.

SERVES 4–6

675 g (1lb 8oz) Rooster or Yukon Gold
    potatoes (or 6 potatoes, preferably
    all similar in size), cut into large,
    even-sized chunks
Vegetable oil, dripping, or goose or
    duck fat
Sea salt

Mum's Roast Potatoes

Preheat the oven to 220°C/425°F/gas mark 7.

Cover the potatoes with cold water in a saucepan, add a pinch of salt and bring to the boil. Reduce the heat, cover and simmer for 8–10 minutes until the outside has just softened. Drain and return to the pan for 1–2 minutes to dry out.

Meanwhile, pour 1cm (½ inch) of oil, dripping or fat into a roasting pan and heat it in the oven or on the hob or stove for a few minutes until it is just smoking. Put the lid back on the potatoes and shake vigorously to break up and soften the edges, or rough up the outside of them with a fork. Tip carefully into the hot oil and baste well.

Place in the oven for 40 minutes, then pour off the majority of the fat before turning the potatoes over. Season to taste with salt and cook for a further 20 minutes until the potatoes are crispy around the edges and golden brown.

To serve, tip the roast potatoes into a warmed serving dish.

Game Crisps

After making your crisps (potato chips) and removing them from the pan, allow the duck fat to cool down, then strain through a fine sieve or strainer. Freeze it for another use.

SERVES 4

300g (1½ cups) duck fat
5 potatoes, scrubbed and cut lengthways into slices about 2mm (¹⁄₁₆ inch) thick.
Sea salt

Heat the duck fat in a heavy-based saucepan set over a medium heat until melted. Add the potatoes in batches (to prevent them from sticking together in the pan) and cook each batch for about 5 minutes. Using a slotted spoon, transfer them to a bowl lined with kitchen paper (paper towels). Serve immediately, sprinkled with sea salt.

Thick Hand-cut Chips

When making chips (fries), dry them with some kitchen paper (paper towels) before cooking because water and oil do not mix. Rapeseed (canola) and sunflower oil have high smoking points and are therefore most suitable for deep-frying. With hand-cut chips, you can choose how thick or thin you'd like them to be. For me, it's always thick, and occasionally cooked in duck fat.

SERVES 4

Oil, for deep-frying
4–6 potatoes (such as Rooster, Maris Piper, Yukon Gold or similar), cut into thick chips (store in water until required)
Salt and vinegar, to serve

Heat the oil in a deep-fat fryer to 170°C (340°F) and add the potato chips. Cook for about 5 minutes until they begin to colour. Remove from the oil and allow to cool for a few minutes.

Heat the oil to 190°C (375°F) and return the chips to it until they are fully cooked – this will take only 1–2 minutes.

Drain the chips on kitchen paper. Sprinkle with salt and a splash of vinegar and serve immediately.

Hasselback Potatoes

These roast potatoes – a Swedish original – have a lovely crispy crust and are a real treat. Making them involves slicing into the potato to create slits, but taking care not to cut right through.

SERVES 4

4 large potatoes, such as Desiree or Russet
2 tbsp olive oil
100g (1 stick) butter, melted
Salt (use fleur de sel if possible) or sea salt
2 tsp chopped oregano

Preheat the oven to 220°C/425°F/gas mark 7.

Cut the potatoes into thin slices without cutting all the way through them. The incisions should go about three-quarters of the way down.

Place the potatoes in a roasting pan, drizzle with olive oil and melted butter and sprinkle with salt and oregano.

Roast for about 40 minutes, basting from time to time.

Crushed Baby Potatoes

This recipe can be adapted to use leftover baby potatoes. Don't overcrush them – they need just a gentle pressing because you don't want the contents to burst from the skins.

SERVES 4–6

1kg (2lb 4oz) baby potatoes
4–5 garlic cloves, unpeeled
70g (5 tbsp) butter
1 tbsp chopped rosemary
1 tbsp chopped flat leaf parsley
Salt and black pepper
30g (⅓ cup) grated Parmesan cheese (optional)

Preheat the oven to 180°C/350°F/gas mark 4.

Place the potatoes into a saucepan of lightly salted boiling water, add the garlic cloves and cook for 18–20 minutes until softened. Drain and place the potatoes and garlic in separate bowls. Gently crush the potatoes with a potato masher and set aside for a moment. Squeeze the garlic out of its skin and mash gently with a fork.

Melt the butter in a small saucepan and add the mashed garlic and the herbs. Season with salt and black pepper.

Toss the crushed potatoes into an ovenproof dish and pour the garlic-and-herb butter over them. Pop into the oven for 10–15 minutes until they are slightly crisp on top. Sprinkle with some grated cheese, if using, before serving.

Something Sweet

Frozen yogurt is my take on the wonderful Italian gelato, which is normally less heavy than conventional ice cream. For the best results, I recommend using an ice cream machine. The berry compote is a delicious accompaniment to the yogurt.

SERVES 6

4 eggs, separated
250ml (1 cup) double (heavy) cream
150g (¾ cup) caster (superfine) sugar
4 tbsp low-fat milk
100ml (½ cup) vanilla yogurt
½ tsp vanilla extract

FOR THE BERRY COMPOTE

200g (2 cups) mixed berries, such as blueberries, raspberries and hulled and halved strawberries
4 tbsp caster (superfine) sugar
2 tbsp Grand Marnier liqueur

Frozen Yogurt Gelato with Berry Compote

If you are not using an ice cream machine, place a large bowl or plastic container in the freezer for about 30 minutes before you begin.

Whisk or beat the egg whites until they form stiff peaks, then set aside while you prepare the 'custard' part of the gelato.

Pour the cream into a third bowl and whisk lightly. Set aside.

Add the sugar to the egg yolks and whisk until the mixture is pale and frothy. Add the milk, yogurt and vanilla extract and combine thoroughly.

Spoon the egg whites into the whipped cream, then fold this mixture gently into the egg yolks using a palette knife or spatula, until all the ingredients are fully incorporated.

Transfer to an ice cream machine and churn according to the manufacturer's instructions. Alternatively, if making by hand, pour the cream mixture into the chilled bowl, cover with a lid or clingfilm (plastic wrap) and freeze for about 1 hour. Whisk the mixture to break up the ice crystals, then return it, covered, to the freezer. Repeat after a further hour. After 3–4 hours, the ice cream is ready.

To make the compote, place the berries in a heavy-based saucepan with the sugar and Grand Marnier, then bring to the boil, stirring, until the sugar dissolves. Continue to boil fast for about 5 minutes until the berries are tender but still holding their shape.

Remove the compote from the heat and transfer it to a bowl. Leave to cool completely, then cover with clingfilm and refrigerate until required. The compote will keep for up to 3 days in the refrigerator.

Remove the gelato from the freezer 15 minutes before serving, then place 1–2 scoops per person in serving bowls. Spoon some berry compote over the gelato.

The floating islands in this dish are wonderfully light and are a lovely texture contrast to the strawberry consommé. Add some basil leaves to the floating islands, if liked.

SERVES 4

250g (9oz) wild strawberries, hulled, plus 8 extra, to serve
400ml (1¾ cups) champagne or prosecco
2 tbsp caster (superfine) sugar
Juice of 1 lemon

FOR THE FLOATING ISLANDS
6 egg whites
Squeeze of lemon juice
120g (⅔ cup) caster (superfine) sugar
1 litre (4¼ cups) milk
1 vanilla pod or bean, split open lengthways

Wild Strawberry Consommé with Floating Islands

First make the floating islands. Whisk the egg whites with a little lemon juice in a large bowl until they form soft peaks. Continuing to beat, add the sugar, a spoonful at a time, until fully incorporated. Set aside.

Meanwhile, heat the milk in a large, shallow saucepan and add the vanilla pod. Bring to the boil, then reduce the heat until the mixture is simmering gently.

Make 8 quenelles (egg shapes) from the meringue mixture by using 2 tablespoons to shape them. Place each quenelle in the simmering milk. Cover with a lid and poach for 6–7 minutes, then remove with a slotted spoon and set aside on kitchen paper (paper towels) to drain.

Place the main quantity of berries in a heatproof glass bowl. Add the champagne, sugar and lemon juice. Cover the bowl with clingfilm (plastic wrap) and place it over a saucepan of simmering water for 15–20 minutes. Strain the liquid through a fine sieve or strainer into a bowl, without crushing the strawberries, to achieve a clear consommé.

Divide the consommé between 4 bowls or glasses, then place 2 quenelles and 2 whole strawberries in each bowl to serve.

Oolong is a semi-fermented tea combining the best characteristics of unoxidized green tea and fully oxidized black tea. The flavour is rich, sweet and fruity, and makes a perfect jelly (gelatin) to accompany the fruit in this dish.

MAKES 4

1 leaf or sheet of gelatine
300ml (1¼ cups) freshly brewed
   oolong tea
2 tbsp caster (superfine) sugar
1 tbsp grated lemon rind

FOR THE RASPBERRY PURÉE
200g (1⅔ cups) raspberries
2 tbsp caster (superfine) sugar
Juice of ½ lemon

FOR THE PASSION FRUIT AND
HONEY YOGURT
2½ leaves or sheets of gelatine
450g (2 cups) natural (plain) yogurt
Pulp from 2 passion fruits
4 tbsp honey

Raspberry and Oolong Tea Jellies with Passion Fruit and Honey Yogurt

First make the raspberry purée. Place the raspberries, caster sugar and lemon juice in a bowl. Using a handheld blender, mix to create a purée. Pass the mixture through a fine sieve or strainer and store it in a covered jar in the refrigerator until needed.

Place the gelatine for the jellies in water and set aside to soak for at least 10 minutes. In a small saucepan set over a medium heat, mix together the tea, 100ml (½ cup) of the raspberry purée and the sugar and stir until the sugar has dissolved. Add the lemon rind and remove the pan from the heat. Drain the gelatine, then stir it into the pan until completely dissolved. Leave the mixture to cool to room temperature. Divide it equally among 4 glasses and position each of them at an angle in a recess of an empty egg carton. Leave to set in the refrigerator for a couple of hours.

When the tea jelly is set, prepare the yogurt layer. Place the gelatine to soak in water for at least 10 minutes. In a small heatproof bowl set over a saucepan of gently simmering water, heat half the yogurt until just warm. Drain the gelatine, then quickly stir it into the warmed yogurt. Immediately add the remaining yogurt, the passion fruit pulp and honey. Without waiting for the mixture to cool down, spoon it on top of the tea jellies, this time positioning the glasses upright. Leave them in the refrigerator to set for at least 2 hours.

Once the yogurt layers have set, serve the desserts with the remaining raspberry purée.

The Italian words *panna cotta* mean 'cooked cream', a very easy dessert to make at home. You simply simmer a mixture of cream, milk and sugar or honey, mix in some gelatine and allow the mixture to cool down and set. It is sure to become a firm family favourite. Use the basic recipe and adapt it to bring in additional flavours according to your personal tastes.

SERVES 4

2 leaves or sheets of gelatine
150ml (⅔ cup) double (heavy) cream
4 tbsp caster (superfine) sugar
1 tsp or 2–3 sprigs heather or lavender
   flowers, tied up in a square of muslin
   (cheesecloth) with kitchen string
1 tsp vanilla extract
300ml (1¼ cups) buttermilk
70g (⅓ cup) Comeragh honey (or
   use any clear honey – acacia honey
   works well), to drizzle

Buttermilk and Heather-infused Panna Cotta with Honey

Soak the gelatine in a bowl of water for at least 10 minutes.

Place the cream, sugar and the bag of flowers in a saucepan set over a medium heat and stir until the sugar dissolves. Bring to a simmer, then set aside for 5 minutes to allow the aroma and flavour of the flowers to infuse the cream.

Remove the bag of flowers. Squeeze the gelatine dry, then stir it into the cream until dissolved. Add in the vanilla extract and buttermilk and stir to combine.

Pour the mixture into 4 glasses and refrigerate for 3 hours or until set. Serve drizzled with the honey.

Sweet and creamy rice puddings easily evoke feelings of nostalgia, harking back to childhood days. You could add a sprinkling of cinnamon or fruit compote to this recipe if you like.

SERVES 6–8

150g (¾ cup) pudding rice or other short-grain rice
450ml (2 cups) milk
150ml (⅔ cup) double (heavy) cream
25g (2 tbsp) butter
4 tbsp caster (superfine) sugar
Seeds from 1 vanilla pod or bean
Freshly whipped cream, to serve (optional)

FOR THE CHOCOLATE CREAM
2 leaves or sheets of gelatine
225ml (1 cup) milk
225ml (1 cup) double (heavy) cream
70g (⅓ cup) honey
225g (8oz) chocolate (at least 70 per cent cocoa solids), broken into pieces
225g (1 cup) natural (plain) yogurt

TO DECORATE (OPTIONAL)
Cocoa powder
4 vanilla pods or beans, snapped in half

Vanilla Rice Pudding and Chocolate Cream

In a saucepan set over a medium heat, bring the rice, milk, cream, butter and sugar to a simmer. Stir in the vanilla seeds and cook for about 20–30 minutes, stirring occasionally, until the rice is tender. Allow to cool for a few minutes, then divide the pudding equally among 6–8 ramekins or glasses. Place in the refrigerator for about 1 hour to set.

Soak the gelatine for the chocolate cream in a bowl of water for at least 10 minutes.

When the puddings have set, bring the milk, cream and honey to a simmer in a large saucepan over a medium heat. Take off the heat and whisk in the chocolate until it has melted.

Squeeze the gelatine dry, then stir into the chocolate mixture until completely dissolved. Add the yogurt and whisk vigorously until well blended. Return the pan to the heat and cook gently for 5 minutes.

Pour a layer of the chocolate cream over each rice pudding. Leave to stand at room temperature for 20 minutes, then refrigerate for at least 4 hours to allow the cream to set properly.

You can decorate the puddings with cocoa powder and half a vanilla pod, if liked, and serve them with whipped cream.

Rich and velvety, these seriously chocolatey fondues are very easy to make and even easier to eat! Serve them with some fresh fruit or marshmallows.

125g (4½oz) dark chocolate, broken
    into small pieces
125g (4½oz) white chocolate, broken
    into small pieces
125g (4½oz) milk chocolate, broken
    into small pieces
375ml (1½ cups) double (heavy) cream
1 tbsp Cointreau liqueur
1 tbsp Irish cream liqueur
600g (1¼lb) strawberries, cut into
    large pieces, to serve

Trio of Chocolate Fondues

Place the 3 types of chocolate in separate bowls.

Place a third of the cream in a saucepan and bring to the boil. Pour the hot cream over the dark chocolate and stir until fully combined; it should be smooth and glossy. Set aside.

Repeat the same process with the white chocolate but this time, when you have your rich chocolate sauce, add the Cointreau. Repeat the process with the milk chocolate, adding the Irish liqueur.

Serve all 3 fondue bowls on one plate with the strawberries to dip into the chocolate.

You will find agar (a vegetarian setting agent) in pharmacies or specialized cook shops. If you've never used it before, bear in mind that it needs to be heated to be effective.

SERVES 4

600ml (2½ cups) unsweetened cloudy apple juice (US apple cider)
100ml (½ cup) cider (US hard cider)
2 tsp five-spice powder
3 cloves
1 cinnamon stick
1 tsp agar
Nutmeg or ground cinnamon, for sprinkling

FOR THE YOGURT MOUSSE
225g (1 cup) natural (plain) yogurt
125ml (½ cup) water
4 tbsp caster (superfine) sugar
½ tsp agar
300ml (1¼ cups) double (heavy) cream, lightly whipped

Spiced Apple Jellies with Yogurt Mousse

In a saucepan, bring the apple juice, cider, five spice, cloves and cinnamon to the boil. Boil, uncovered, for 15 minutes or until the juice has reduced to about 500ml (2 cups). Set aside to cool for 15 minutes.

Strain the cooled mixture through a muslin-lined sieve or cheesecloth-lined strainer into a clean saucepan. Place the pan on the heat and sprinkle in the agar. Bring the mixture to the boil, then simmer very gently for 2 minutes, stirring once or twice.

Pour the mixture into 4 glasses or ramekins and allow to cool, then chill for at least 2 hours.

In the meantime, make the mousse. Place the yogurt in a bowl and whisk it until it is smooth.

In a small saucepan, combine the water, sugar and agar and bring to the boil. Reduce the heat and simmer for 2 minutes, stirring once or twice. Then, working quickly, whisk the hot mixture into the yogurt. Add the whipped cream and whisk just until combined. Put the mousse into a piping (pastry) bag or a bowl and place in the refrigerator to chill for at least 2 hours.

Pipe or spoon a dollop of mousse onto each jelly and sprinkle with freshly grated nutmeg or cinnamon.

My version of Eton Mess. Combining melting meringue with two types of berries and lemon curd make it burst with flavour. Try it with the basil oil – you won't regret it.

SERVES 4

4 egg whites
240g (1¼ cups) caster (superfine) sugar
½ tsp cornflour (cornstarch)
½ tsp white wine vinegar

FOR THE LEMON CURD
Grated rind and juice of 2 lemons
4 large (US extra-large) eggs
115g (⅔ cup) caster (superfine) sugar
115g (1 stick) cold butter, cubed

TO SERVE
225g (1¾ cups) raspberries
225g (1½ cups) strawberries, halved
Juice of ½ lemon
1–2 tbsp Basil Oil (see page 209)

Kinky Eton Mess

Preheat the oven to 120°C/250°F/gas mark ½. Line a 33 x 23cm (13 x 9-inch) baking sheet or meringue tray with nonstick baking paper

Place the egg whites in a spotlessly clean bowl and whisk at full speed until stiff.

Whisking more slowly, add the sugar, a little at a time. When all incorporated, add the cornflour and vinegar and give a final whisk at high speed. The mixture should be glossy and, when turned upside-down, remain in the bowl.

Scoop the mixture onto the baking sheet and spread it out evenly to a thickness of about 3cm (1¼ inches). Bake for 1 hour, until the meringue is very firm to the touch but still soft in the middle. I normally leave mine to cool in the oven with the door propped ajar.

While the meringue is cooling, put all the lemon curd ingredients except the butter into a heatproof bowl and place over a saucepan of simmering water. Whisk continuously by hand until the mixture thickens, then slowly whisk in the butter, piece by piece, and cook for 10–12 minutes until it thickens further. Set aside to cool.

Place the berries, lemon juice and basil oil in a bowl and toss together.

To serve, lightly break up the meringue and mix with the berries and lemon curd in a presentation bowl or in 4 glasses.

This light, zesty dessert is the perfect palate cleanser after a meal.

SERVE 6–8

4 leaves or sheets of gelatine
500ml (2 cups) water
850ml (3½ cups) double (heavy) cream
3 eggs, separated
100g (½ cup) caster (superfine) sugar
Grated rind and juice of 1 lemon
Whipped cream, to serve (optional)

FOR THE CANDIED ZEST
4 tbsp caster (superfine) sugar
Grated rind of 2 lemons
Juice of ½ lemon

Lemon Mousse with Candied Zest

Put the gelatine leaves and the water into a small bowl and set aside for at least 10 minutes.

Pour the cream into a large bowl and whisk until soft peaks form.

In a separate bowl, whisk together the egg yolks, sugar and lemon rind, then whisk in the lemon juice. Pour into the cream and whisk together.

In a large bowl, whisk the egg whites until they form stiff peaks.

Put the gelatine and half its water into a small saucepan set over a medium heat and swirl the contents in the pan until the gelatine has dissolved. Whisk into the cream mixture, then fold in the egg whites.

Pour the mousse into 6–8 serving moulds or glasses and chill in the refrigerator for at least 1 hour until set.

Meanwhile, make the candied zest. Put all the ingredients into a small saucepan set over a medium heat and cook for about 5 minutes, until the mixture becomes a sticky syrup. Transfer to a bowl and set aside to cool at room temperature.

To serve, if using moulds, invert the mousses onto plates and drizzle the zest around each one. If using serving glasses, put a quenelle (see page 172) of whipped cream in the centre of each mousse and top with a little candied zest.

Elderflowers are in season during June and July. Wash the flower heads well before use, especially those that have been picked from the roadside.

SERVES 4

900g (6 cups) fresh gooseberries,
    topped and tailed or trimmed
    (or 900g/4 cups canned gooseberries)
Flower heads from 2–3 elderflower stems
140g (¾ cup) caster (superfine) sugar
150ml (⅔ cup) water
400ml (1¾ cups) double (heavy) cream

Elderflower and Gooseberry Layered Fool

Place the gooseberries, elderflowers and sugar in a saucepan with the water and bring to the boil. Reduce the heat and simmer for 10 minutes until the fruits have softened. Remove the flowers, then set the mixture aside and allow to cool completely.

In a large bowl, whip the cream until thickened.

In 4 glasses, alternate layers of whipped cream and fruit purée, finishing with a swirl of the cream. Chill in the refrigerator for at least 15 minutes.

Serve alone or with some shortbread biscuits or cookies.

Pink Lady apples are a great alternative to the local varieties I like to use. When transferring uncooked pastry, I would normally roll it over a rolling pin to support it, then transfer it to the desired surface – a technique that saves a few tears.

SERVES 4

300g (10½oz) ready-made sweetened
    shortcrust pastry (pie dough)
Juice of 1 lemon
6–8 Kerry Pippin, Pink Lady or other
    apples
200g (1¾ sticks) butter, melted
70g (⅓ cup) brown sugar
2 tbsp honey

Simple Apple Tart

Preheat the oven to 200°C/400°F/gas mark 6. Line a baking sheet with nonstick baking paper.

On a lightly floured work surface, roll the sweet pastry into a circle about 28cm (11 inches) in diameter and 3mm (1/8 inch) thick. Place on the baking sheet and prick all over with a fork. Transfer it, uncovered, to the refrigerator for about 10 minutes (chilling prevents it from shrinking during cooking).

Put the lemon juice in a large bowl. Peel, core and thinly slice the apples, tossing the slices in the lemon juice as soon as you have cut them to prevent the flesh from discolouring.

Brush the chilled pastry with some of the melted butter. Arrange the apples on it in overlapping concentric circles. Brush with half of the butter, then sprinkle with the sugar. Bake for about 10 minutes, then brush with the remaining butter and drizzle with the honey before baking for another 10 minutes.

Remove the tart from the oven and leave to cool, then serve with a scoop or 2 of your favourite ice cream, if liked.

Making marshmallows is fun, but do be careful with the sugar and glucose syrup mixture when it's hot. There are many possible variations, but I suggest you start with this basic recipe and take it from there.

SERVES 4

9 leaves or sheets of gelatine, soaked in in water for about 10 minutes, then squeezed dry
450g (2¼ cups) caster (superfine) sugar
1 tbsp liquid glucose
200ml (1 cup) water

Seeds from 1 vanilla pod or bean
2 egg whites
1 tsp sunflower oil
Cornflour (cornstarch), for dusting
Icing (confectioners') sugar, for dusting
3 peaches, peeled, stoned (pitted) and thickly sliced
Butterscotch Sauce (see page 210)

Peach and Marshmallow Skewers with Butterscotch Sauce

Place the sugar, glucose and water in a heavy-based saucepan. Bring to the boil and continue to cook until the temperature reaches 127°C (260°F) on a sugar (candy) thermometer. Add the vanilla seeds, then stir in the gelatine until dissolved.

Whisk the egg whites in a large bowl until soft peaks form. Slowly whisk in the hot sugar mixture until the whites thicken and become very glossy. Continue whisking for about 5 minutes, or until stiff peaks form.

Take a roasting pan about 40 x 25cm (16 x 10 inches) and 5cm (2 inches) deep and very lightly brush it with sunflower oil, then dust with cornflour and icing sugar. Pour in the marshmallow mixture and spread it evenly with a palette knife or spatula. Leave to set at room temperature for at least 1 hour.

Once the marshmallow is set, turn it out onto a work surface dusted with cornflour and icing sugar and, with a hot knife, cut it into 2cm (¾-inch) cubes.

To serve, thread the peach pieces and marshmallow cubes onto skewers and caramelize them on a barbecue. Alternatively, lay the skewers on a greased baking sheet and place under a preheated grill (broiler) for 2 minutes, then turn over the skewers and grill for another 2 minutes or until caramelized. Drizzle with a little butterscotch sauce and serve immediately with extra butterscotch sauce for dipping.

Harvey Wallbanger Smoothie with Vanilla Float

This is my take on the classic 1960s cocktail known as the Harvey Wallbanger, reportedly named after a party guest named Harvey who banged his head on the wall after a few too many.

MAKES ABOUT 500ML (2 CUPS)

4 tbsp vodka
200ml (1 cup) freshly squeezed orange juice
2 tbsp Galliano liqueur
200g (1 cup) ice cubes, crushed
Vanilla ice cream (1 scoop per serving)
1 orange, sliced, to decorate

Place all the ingredients except the ice cream into a smoothie maker or blender and blitz until they are combined. Serve with a scoop of ice cream and decorate with orange slices.

Banana and Berry Smoothie with Vanilla Float

Making this smoothie is a perfect way to use up fruits that are getting overripe: just pop them in the food processor and blitz to a purée. You can use any variation of soft fruits. Remember that frozen fruits work just as well.

MAKES ABOUT 500ML (2 CUPS)

1 banana
100g (⅔ cup) strawberries, hulled and halved
4 sprigs of tarragon
200g (1 cup) ice cubes, crushed
125ml (½ cup) vanilla yogurt
Vanilla ice cream (1 scoop per serving)

Purée the banana, strawberries and tarragon in a food processor, then add the ice and yogurt and whiz again until creamy. Serve with a scoop of ice cream.

I promise that this crumble is the crunchiest you'll ever have tasted!

SERVES 6

3½ tbsp caster (superfine) sugar
Finely grated rind and juice of 1 small
  orange
225g (8oz) Granny Smith, Cox or
  Pippin apples, peeled, cored and
  cut into slices
225g (1½ cups) blackberries
Crème fraîche, to serve

FOR THE CRUMBLE TOPPING

50g (⅓ cup) plain (all-purpose) flour
50g (⅓ cup) wholemeal (whole-wheat)
  flour
½ tsp baking powder
4 tbsp muscovado or dark brown sugar
70g (⅔ cup) mixed nuts, finely chopped
50g (½ cup) oatmeal (oat bran)
1 tbsp orange marmalade or Orange
  Irish Whiskey Marmalade (see
  page 211)
50g (4 tbsp) butter, cut into cubes

Apple and Blackberry Marmalade Crumble

Preheat the oven to 180°C/350°F/gas mark 4.

First make the crumble topping. Sift the flours and baking powder into a bowl,
then tip the residue from the sifter back into the bowl. Stir in the muscovado sugar,
mixed nuts, oatmeal and marmalade. Rub in the butter until the mixture resembles
breadcrumbs. Place on a baking sheet and bake for 10–15 minutes until the mixture
is golden brown.

Meanwhile, put the caster sugar, orange rind and juice into a saucepan. Bring
to the boil and continue boiling until the mixture reaches a light caramel colour.

Add the apples, cover with a lid, then simmer for 3–5 minutes until the fruit is
tender but still holding its shape. Remove from the heat and add the blackberries.

Transfer the fruit mixture to an ovenproof dish and sprinkle the crumble on top.
Bake for another 15 minutes, until the topping is crisp and golden brown.

Serve with crème fraîche.

Thick, creamy and packing a nice kick of alcohol, this drink is the perfect Christmas beverage.

4 eggs, separated
120g (⅔ cup) caster (superfine) sugar
½ tsp ground or freshly grated nutmeg
500ml (2 cups) double (heavy) cream
300ml (1¼ cups) full-fat (whole) milk
100ml (½ cup) dark rum
100ml (½ cup) brandy

Indulgent Eggnog

In a bowl, beat the egg yolks until pale and very frothy. Add the sugar and continue beating, then mix in the nutmeg. Add the cream, a little at a time, then add the milk a little at a time. Finally, beat in the rum and brandy.

In a separate bowl, whisk the egg whites until they form stiff peaks. Fold them into the yolk mixture, ensuring they are fully incorporated.

Give your arms a break from all that beating and put the eggnog in the refrigerator to chill for 1–2 hours.

Instead of using the traditional slices of bread, I like to use croissants for this pudding as they create a light dish. Serve with jugs of Butterscotch Sauce (see page 210) and Crème Anglaise (see page 210) so that everyone can help themselves.

SERVES 4–6

70g (5 tbsp) softened butter, for
    greasing
6–8 croissants (crescent rolls), cut into
    large pieces
50g (⅓ cup) raisins
300ml (1¼ cups) double (heavy)
    cream
300ml (1¼ cups) milk
4 eggs
½ tsp ground cinnamon
70g (⅓ cup) caster (superfine) sugar

Croissant Bread and Butter Pudding

Generously butter an ovenproof dish that measures about 20 x 30cm (8 x 12 inches).

Arrange a single layer of croissant chunks, slightly overlapping, in the bottom of the dish. Scatter over some of the raisins, place another layer of croissant chunks on top and scatter over the remaining raisins. Press down gently with a fish slice or spatula.

To make the custard, heat the cream and milk in a saucepan until the mixture comes almost to the boil. Remove from the heat. Meanwhile, whisk together the eggs, ground cinnamon and sugar in a large heatproof bowl set over a saucepan of simmering water until the mixture is thickened and the whisk or beaters leave a trail when lifted. Remove from the heat and beat in the cream mixture until well combined.

Pour two-thirds of the custard over the croissants and leave to stand for about 30 minutes or until they have soaked up all the liquid. Preheat the oven to 180°C/350°F/gas mark 4.

Pour the remaining custard over the soaked croissants and press down firmly with a fish slice or spatula so that the custard reaches halfway up the croissants. Place the dish in a roasting pan and pour in enough water to come a third of the way up the side of the dish. Bake for 30–35 minutes until the custard is just set and the top is golden brown. Serve immediately.

Amarena cherries, which are the cherries I like to use for this recipe, are little bombs of flavour. The syrupy juices transform the fruit into a sweet and sour delight.

SERVES 6–8

4 egg yolks
115g (⅔ cup) caster (superfine) sugar
225g (1 cup) mascarpone cheese
200ml (1 cup) pouring (light) cream,
  lightly whipped
1 double espresso or 1 cup of strong
  coffee
100ml (½ cup) Marsala or other
  medium-sweet red wine
18–24 sponge fingers
  (ladyfinger cookies)
100g (⅔ cup) canned Amarena cherries
50g (½ cup) cocoa powder

Cherry Tiramisu

Beat together the egg yolks and sugar for 4–5 minutes until very pale and creamy, then beat in the mascarpone cheese. Fold in the whipped cream and set aside.

Mix the coffee and Marsala together in a bowl.

Select a shallow serving dish (or individual decorative glasses – wine or Martini glasses are ideal).

Dip the sponge fingers into the coffee mixture one by one and arrange half of them flat in the serving dish. Place a few cherries on top. Spread half of the creamy mixture over them, then make another layer of biscuits, cherries and cream mixture in the same way. Smooth the surface with a warm palette knife or spatula. Dust with the cocoa powder and decorate with the remaining cherries. Transfer to the refrigerator and chill for 2–3 hours.

This dessert is a very fresh and tasty summer option. I love the light, fluffy sponge. If desired, you can bake the mixture in a 900g (9 x 5 x 3-inch) loaf tin, but you will need to adjust the cooking time to about 50–60 minutes.

SERVES 8

225g (2 sticks) softened butter
225g (1 cup + 2 tbsp) caster
    (superfine) sugar
Grated rind of 2 lemons
4 large (US extra-large) eggs
225g (1¾ cups) self-raising flour
    (or 1¾ cups all-purpose flour mixed
    with 1¾ tsp baking powder)

FOR THE FILLING
Grated rind and juice of 1 lemon
2 eggs
100g (½ cup) caster (superfine) sugar
55g (4 tbsp) cold butter, cubed

FOR THE TOPPING
500ml (2 cups) double (heavy) cream,
    beaten until stiff
250g (1⅔ cups) strawberries, hulled
    and halved

Lemon Curd Sponge with Strawberries

Preheat the oven to 180°C/350°F/gas mark 4. Grease and line 2 x 20cm (8-inch) sandwich cake tins with greaseproof (wax) paper or nonstick baking paper.

First make the filling. Put all ingredients except the butter into a heatproof bowl set over a saucepan of simmering water. Whisk continuously by hand until the mixture thickens, then slowly beat in the butter, piece by piece, and cook for 10–12 minutes until the mixture thickens further. Set aside to cool.

To make the cake batter, beat the butter and sugar in a large mixing bowl until light and fluffy. Stir in the lemon rind, then mix in the eggs and flour. If you find the mixture is a little dry, you can add a tablespoon of milk to loosen it up.

Divide the mixture between the prepared cake tins and bake for 20–25 minutes or until a skewer or toothpick inserted in the centre comes out clean. Allow the cakes to cool in their tins on a wire rack, then turn them out.

Place 1 sponge layer on a serving platter and spread most of the filling on it. Top with the second sponge layer and spread the remaining filling on it. Pipe some cream swirls on top and decorate with the berries.

This tangy orange pudding will delight your taste buds, but don't be tempted to open the oven while it's baking or you may not get the rise you want.

SERVES 8–10

275g (2½ sticks) butter, plus extra for greasing
4 tbsp demerara or other raw sugar
3 oranges, peeled, pith removed and segmented
1 orange, peeled, pith removed and thinly sliced
115g (1 cup) self-raising flour (or 1 cup all-purpose flour and increase the baking powder to 2 tsp)

1 tsp baking powder
175g (¾ cup) caster (superfine) sugar
2 eggs
3 tsp milk

TO SERVE
250ml (1 cup) double (heavy) cream
Seeds from 1 vanilla pod or bean

Orange Pudding

Preheat the oven to 180°C/350°F/gas mark 4. Butter an ovenproof dish or cake tin with a diameter of about 20cm (8 inches).

Melt 100g (1 stick) of the butter in a saucepan over a low heat, add the demerara sugar and cook until slightly caramelized. Add the orange segments and cook over a medium heat for 6–8 minutes until they are caramelized.

Arrange the orange slices in the bottom of the prepared dish and pour over the caramelized oranges and sauce.

Sift the flour and baking powder into a bowl. In a separate bowl, beat together the remaining butter and caster sugar until fluffy and light. Don't rush this stage. Beat in the eggs, one by one, with a little of the sifted flour. Fold in the remaining flour and mix in the milk.

Spoon the mixture over the oranges and bake for 30–40 minutes until the sponge is golden.

Pour the cream into a bowl, add the vanilla seeds and whip to soft peaks. Serve the pudding hot or cold with the vanilla cream.

Porter cake incorporates stout, such as Guinness or Murphys, so it is beautifully rich, and the flavour develops as it matures. However, you'll find that these lollies (lollipops) won't hang around.

MAKES 12–20 MINI LOLLIPOPS

450g (3 cups) sultanas (golden raisins)
70g (⅓ cup) mixed candied peel,
    chopped
300ml (1¼ cups) porter or Guinness
Nonstick baking spray
500g (4 cups) plain (all-purpose) flour
1 tsp ground nutmeg
1½ tsp ground mixed spice (allspice)
2 tsp baking powder
Pinch of salt
275g (2½ sticks) butter
225g (1 cup) light soft brown sugar
2 eggs

Porter Cake Lollies

Place the sultanas and mixed peel in a bowl with the porter or Guinness and leave to soak overnight, if possible.

Preheat the oven to 160°C/325°F/gas mark 3. Spray 2 x 8-section cake lollipop silicone moulds or deep muffin tins with nonstick baking spray.

Sift the flour, nutmeg, mixed spice, baking powder and salt into a large bowl. Rub in the butter, then stir in the sugar. Form a well in the centre of the mixture.

In a second bowl, whisk the eggs, then pour them into the well in the centre of the flour mixture. Gradually incorporate the dry ingredients into the whisked egg, slowly pouring in the porter or Guinness mixture at the same time.

Transfer the mixture to the prepared moulds, filling them to two-thirds capacity, and bake for about 20 minutes or until a skewer or toothpick inserted into the centre comes out clean. Allow to cool for about 20 minutes before turning out onto a wire rack. Insert a wooden skewer or lollipop stick into the centre of each mini cake.

If using muffin tins, insert lollipop sticks into the cakes halfway through the cooking time so they will set. Cool as above.

Orange Cream Biscuits

These shortbread crumbly biscuits (cookies) are a real treat.

MAKES 36 SANDWICH BISCUITS

100g (½ cup) cream cheese
240g (2 sticks) softened butter
Finely grated rind and juice of ½ orange
225g (1 cup + 2 tbsp) caster (superfine) sugar
1 egg yolk
1 tsp vanilla extract
340g (3¾ cups) plain (all-purpose) flour
Icing (confectioners') sugar, to dust

FOR THE BUTTERCREAM FILLING
115g (1 stick) softened butter
200g (1⅔ cups) icing sugar, plus extra for dusting
Finely grated rind of ½ orange
2 tbsp orange juice

Preheat the oven to 180°C/350°F/gas mark 4. Line several baking sheets with nonstick baking paper.

In a large bowl, and using an electric mixer, beat together the cream cheese, butter, orange juice and rind, sugar, egg yolk and vanilla extract until light and creamy. Sift in the flour and combine to achieve a smooth batter.

Spoon the mixture into a large piping or pastry bag fitted with a 4cm (1½-inch) star nozzle and pipe 72 stars on the baking sheets, spacing them about 5cm (2 inches) apart. Bake for 20 minutes until golden, then use a palette knife or spatula to transfer them to wire racks. Leave to cool

To make the cream filling, beat together the butter, sugar, orange rind and juice until smooth.

Place half of the biscuits upside-down on your work surface and place a teaspoonful of filling on each one. Place another biscuit on top and press down gently. Leave in a cool place until set, then dust with icing sugar before serving.

Wine Biscuits

Originally from Italy, these biscuits (cookies) have a subtle wine taste and aren't too sweet. Try them with your favourite cheese and a nice glass of fruity wine.

MAKES 20–24 BISCUITS

350g (2¾ cups) plain (all-purpose) flour
1 tsp baking powder
4 tbsp brown sugar
½ tsp ground cinnamon
4 tbsp vegetable oil
½ tsp vanilla extract
110ml (½ cup) dry red wine
60g (⅓ cup) granulated sugar

Preheat the oven to 180°C/350F/gas mark 4. Line a baking sheet with nonstick baking paper.

In a large bowl, combine the flour, baking powder, brown sugar and cinnamon. Mix in the oil and vanilla extract, then add the wine (if added sooner it will be absorbed solely by the flour). Mix to form a dough. Then roll into a log about 5cm (2 inches) in diameter. Wrap it in clingfilm (plastic wrap) and chill for at least 1 hour.

Slice the dough into circles that are about 2cm (¾ inch) thick. Roll them in granulated sugar and place on the prepared baking sheet.

Bake for 25 minutes or until slightly brown. Cool on a wire rack until crisp.

Storecupboard, Sauces and Stocks

Béchamel Sauce

Béchamel is a basic white sauce to which you can add your own herbs and seasoning. Try adding a handful of parsley to make a parsley sauce for your ham or fish dishes. Alternatively, add some grated cheese and 1 egg yolk to make a delicious sauce to accompany fish.

MAKES ABOUT 500ML (2 CUPS)

30g (2 tbsp) butter
40g (⅓ cup) plain (all-purpose) flour
500ml (2 cups) milk
1 onion, studded with cloves
1 carrot, sliced
1 bouquet garni
Salt and black pepper

Melt the butter in a saucepan over a gentle heat, add the flour and stir with a wooden spoon until the mixture becomes pale. Set the roux aside.

Place the milk, onion, carrot and bouquet garni in a saucepan and simmer gently for 4–6 minutes to infuse the flavours. Strain the milk into the roux, discarding the onion, carrot and bouquet garni. Return the pan to the heat stirring constantly until the sauce has thickened.

Season with salt and black pepper, then use as required. The sauce can be stored for up to 2 days in the refrigerator.

Tarragon Butter Sauce

Tarragon is a delicate green herb that has a distinctive aniseed flavour. This sauce is perfect with chicken or fish dishes.

MAKES 225ML (1 CUP)

1 shallot, finely chopped
Juice of 1 lemon
Salt and black pepper
4 tsp double (heavy) cream
200g (1¾ tbsp) cold butter, cut into pieces
1 tbsp finely chopped tarragon

In a saucepan set over a medium heat, combine the shallot and lemon juice and season with salt. Bring the mixture to a simmer and pour in the cream. Simmer for a further 2 minutes.

Remove from the heat and whisk in the butter, a couple of pieces at a time. Stir in the chopped tarragon, then season with salt and black pepper.

Serve immediately, or keep the sauce warm until needed.

Hollandaise Sauce

There are a number of approaches to making hollandaise sauce, and this version is my take on the classic recipe. Traditionally, it is served with fish or is an integral part of the finger-lickingly good eggs Benedict. Regardless of how many times you have made hollandaise sauce, you must still employ the same level of care and precision: mistakes can easily be made. That being said, don't be put off making it because, if you follow the steps below, it will work out perfectly.

MAKES ABOUT 350ML (1½ CUPS)

225g (2 sticks) clarified butter (see box)
2 tbsp lemon juice
3 large (US extra-large) egg yolks
White pepper

Melt the butter in a saucepan over a gentle heat, then set aside.

Place a heatproof bowl over a pan of simmering water. Pour in the lemon juice, then add the egg yolks and beat continuously until light and creamy. You need to be very careful at this stage because the line between creamy and scrambled is very fine.

Remove the bowl from the heat, then pour in the melted butter while continuing to whisk constantly. If, after adding all the butter, the sauce is still a little thick for your liking, whisk in a couple of tablespoons of boiling water and a squeeze of lemon. Season with white pepper to taste.

HOW TO MAKE CLARIFIED BUTTER

Melt the butter in a small pan over a low heat. Leave to stand for a few minutes until all the oil rises to the top, then skim off any scum. Spoon the remaining oil into a sealable plastic container, ensuring no sediment is present. The clarified butter will keep in the refrigerator for up 2 months.

Mint Sauce

Mint sauce is perfect with roast lamb, which is probably why the two are traditionally paired. But try adding a spoonful to some natural (plain) yogurt for a light, refreshing accompaniment to a spicy curry.

MAKES 125ML (½ CUP)

150g (3 cups) mint leaves
1 tsp caster (superfine) sugar
100ml (½ cup) white or rice vinegar
2 tbsp warm water

Place the mint and sugar in the bowl of a food processor. Add the vinegar and water and blitz the mixture until all the mint has been shredded. Serve immediately.

Bread Sauce

Bread sauce is an ideal accompaniment to turkey or any poultry. It's well worth the effort of making your own because shop-bought bread sauce just doesn't taste the same.

MAKES 550ML (2⅓ CUPS)

450ml (2 cups) milk
1 small onion, studded with 4 cloves
2 bay leaves
115g (2 cups) fresh white breadcrumbs
Salt and black pepper
½ tsp freshly grated nutmeg
50g (2 tbsp) butter
4 tsp double (heavy) cream

Pour the milk into a saucepan, add the clove-studded onion and the bay leaves and gently bring to the boil. Remove the onion and bay leaves, then sprinkle in the breadcrumbs and season with salt and black pepper. Cook on a very gentle heat for 8–10 minutes.

Stir in the nutmeg, butter and cream, which will flavour and enrich the sauce even further. Cook for another 5–10 minutes, then transfer to a sauceboat and serve immediately.

Turkey Gravy

Everyone has their own recipe for turkey gravy. This is one of my favourites, which can be prepared in advance and reheated later.

MAKES ABOUT 400–500ML (1¾–2 CUPS)

Turkey giblets
2 carrots, chopped
1 onion, chopped
1 tbsp olive oil
Salt and black pepper
700ml (3 cups) turkey or chicken stock
2 bay leaves
4 tbsp plain (all-purpose) flour
150ml (⅔ cup) red wine
50g (4 tbsp) butter, cubed

Preheat the oven to 180°C/350°F/gas mark 4.

Place the turkey giblets, carrots and onion in a roasting pan and drizzle with the olive oil. Season with salt and black pepper. Roast for 45–60 minutes until the giblets are cooked through. Drain off any excess fat, if there is any, and set the pan aside.

Pour the turkey stock into a saucepan, add the bay leaves and bring to the boil.

Place the pan of giblets on the hob or stove. Sprinkle in the flour and brown it over a moderate heat. Pour in the wine to deglaze the pan, scraping up the bits from the base of the pan, and stir for 1 minute. Pour in the stock and stir well. Pass the gravy through a sieve or strainer into a fresh saucepan.

Bring the liquid to the boil and cook until the gravy has reduced by half. Stir the butter cubes into the gravy – these will give it extra flavour and an attractive gloss. Serve immediately.

Dalkey Mustard Dressing

I make this dressing by simply shaking together the ingredients in a clean screw-top jar. It can also be whisked in a bowl, but I find the jar an excellent container for storage.

MAKES ABOUT 100ML (½ CUP)

Juice of ½ lemon
Pinch of caster (superfine) sugar
Salt and black pepper
6 tbsp olive oil
1 tbsp Dalkey mustard (or use wholegrain mustard)

Place the lemon juice in a screw-top jar, add the sugar and a good pinch of salt, then shake until the salt has dissolved.

Add the oil and mustard to the jar and shake again until it forms a thick emulsion. Season with salt and black pepper to taste and chill until needed.

Wild Garlic Pesto

Wild garlic is a forager's delight, found in woodlands from early spring to the end of May. Try using coriander (cilantro) as an alternative if you find wild garlic, hard to locate.

MAKES ABOUT 500ML (2 CUPS)

300g (10½oz) wild garlic (about 1 large handful of cloves)
15g (½oz) Parmesan cheese, grated
Juice of ½ lemon
½ tsp coriander seeds, crushed
250ml (9fl oz) olive oil
Salt and black pepper

Whiz all the ingredients in a food processor, or purée with a handheld blender, until the mixture is smooth.

The pesto will keep in the refrigerator for up to 3 weeks. Although it will darken slightly in colour over time, it will still be delicious – the flavours will just be more mature.

Balsamic Reduction

Balsamic reduction is a good condiment to have in your larder or pantry. It adds a nice element to most salads and works particularly well with fish. It will keep for up to 6 months in a cool, dark place, but if you prefer to store it in the refrigerator, take it out for about 30 minutes prior to serving to bring it up to room temperature, or put the bottle on the table in a bowl of hot water.

MAKES ABOUT 150ML (⅓ CUP)

200ml (1 cup) balsamic vinegar
2 tbsp brown sugar or honey

Put both ingredients in a saucepan over a very low heat and stir to combine. Bring to a gentle boil, then simmer for 6–8 minutes until the mixture becomes thick and syrupy.

Transfer the mixture to a sterilized bottle (see box) and use as required.

HOW TO STERILIZE BOTTLES AND JARS FOR PRESERVING

Preheat the oven to 140°C/275°F/gas mark 1. Wash and rinse your bottles and/or jars and lids several times with boiling water. Transfer them to the empty preheated oven and leave to dry for 20 minutes. Alternatively, wash the bottles, jars and lids on the hottest cycle in your dishwasher.

Basil Oil

Basil is one of my favourite herbs, and whenever I have a large quantity to hand, I like to make a batch of this basil oil. It is a lovely taste of the Mediterranean.

MAKES ABOUT 225ML (1 CUP)

500g (1lb 2oz) basil
300g (10½oz) flat leaf parsley
200ml (1 cup) grapeseed oil

Pick through the basil and parsley leaves, removing any that are discoloured.

Bring a saucepan of water to the boil. Place a bowl of iced water nearby.

Put the herbs in the boiling water and blanch for about 1 minute, then transfer them to the iced water for about 3 minutes– this helps to retain their brightness and flavour. Remove with a slotted spoon and lightly pat dry with kitchen paper (paper towels).

Place the herbs in a bowl and a drizzle with a little of the oil. Using a handheld blender, blitz the mixture, then continue blitzing as you add the remaining oil in a constant stream. Leave to infuse for about 20 minutes before passing the mixture through muslin or cheesecloth into a jug or pitcher. Transfer the oil into a sterilized jar (see box).

Store in the refrigerator for up to 2 weeks and bring to room temperature before using. Alternatively, freeze small quantities in large freezing bags on a flat surface (they take less room to store) and serve the frozen oil straight from the freezer on a hot meat, fish or dessert.

Crème Anglaise

Crème Anglaise is a flourless custard.
Be cautious when cooking this sauce –
if you overheat it, it will lose its elegance.

MAKES 600–700ML (2½–3 CUPS)

1 vanilla pod or bean, split open lengthways
500ml (2 cups) double (heavy) cream
6 egg yolks
120g (⅔ cup) caster (superfine) sugar

Put the vanilla pod and the cream into a large
saucepan over a medium heat and bring to the
boil. Set aside for about 15 minutes to infuse.

Beat together the egg yolks and sugar until thick,
then add the vanilla-infused cream.

Return the entire mixture to the pan and heat
gently, stirring continuously, until the custard has
thickened and coats the back of the spoon. Pass
it through a fine sieve or strainer.

Serve warm or cold.

Butterscotch Sauce

This sauce is so easy to make and it is
perfect with ice cream or as a dip for
fresh fruit. The primary flavours are no
more than brown sugar and cream.

MAKES 300ML (1¼ CUPS)

50g (4 tbsp) butter
4 tbsp brown sugar
250ml (1 cup) pouring (light) cream

Melt the butter in a saucepan, add in the brown
sugar and bring to the boil. (Sugar has a very high
boiling point, so take care not to burn yourself.)

Pour in the cream, whisking continuously,
and bring to the boil. Reduce the heat to a
gentle simmer and cook for 8–10 minutes.
Serve immediately.

Orange Irish Whiskey Marmalade

The best time to make orange marmalade is during the winter, but you can also make this recipe with any citrus fruit. Try blood oranges, grapefruits, mandarins or kumquats.

MAKES 4 X 250G (8-OZ) JARS

1kg (2lb) oranges, unpeeled and quartered
250ml (1 cup) fresh orange juice
1kg (5 cups) caster (superfine) sugar
1 measure Jameson whiskey
Juice of 2 lemons, sieved to remove any pips

Place the oranges in a food processor (in batches if necessary) with some of the juice and pulse until the fruit has broken down and formed a pulp.

Place the orange pulp, sugar and whiskey in a large saucepan. Add the lemon juice and the remaining orange juice and mix thoroughly.

Place the saucepan on a moderate heat and bring to a boil for 3 minutes, then simmer for about 5–8 minutes, stirring frequently to prevent the marmalade from sticking to the bottom of the pan.

Check if the marmalde is ready to set (see box), then pour it into warmed, sterilized preserving or canning jars (see page 209) and seal immediately. Label, date and store in a cool dark place for up to 9 months.

If you live in a country that recommends processing preserves in a water bath for long-term storage, refer to online sources for advice.

Blackberry Jam

We all love blackberries, a delicious summer fruit with a deep colour and equally intense flavour, so this jam makes a welcome addition to a storecupboard.

MAKES 500G (1⅔ CUPS)

1kg (7 cups) blackberries
1kg (5 cups) caster (superfine) sugar
Juice of 1 lemon

Place the blackberries and sugar in a clean saucepan. Strain in the lemon juice, mix thoroughly and bring to the boil, stirring occasionally.

Reduce the heat to a gentle simmer and continue to cook for 12–15 minutes until the jam is ready to set (see box). Pour the jam into warmed, sterilized preserving or canning jars (see page 209) and seal immediately. Label, date and store in a cool dark place for up to 9 months.

If you live in a country that recommends processing preserves in a water bath for long-term storage, refer to online sources for advice.

HOW TO CHECK FOR SET

Before you begin making your jam or jelly, place some saucers in the refrigerator to chill for about an hour. When it's time to check the set of your jam, place a spoonful of it on a chilled saucer and return it to the refrigerator for 5 minutes. Cooked jam will set on the saucer within 4–5 minutes.

Rhubarb and Grape Jam

This is a great way to use end-of-season rhubarb and grapes.

MAKE 7 X 250G (8-OZ) JARS

500g (1lb 2oz) young ruby rhubarb, cut into 2cm (¾-inch) lengths
500g (1lb 2oz) seedless green grapes, halved
Grated rind and juice of 1 orange
250g (1¼ cups) caster (superfine) sugar
500g (2½ cups) brown sugar
100ml (½ cup) water
10ml (2 tsp) liquid pectin or 2 tsp powdered pectin mixed with 1 tsp caster (superfine) sugar

Place the rhubarb, grapes, orange rind and juice and 100g (½ cup) of the caster sugar in a large, heavy-based saucepan. Leave to marinate for at least 1 hour.

Add the remaining caster sugar, the brown sugar and water and bring to a simmer over a medium heat. When the sugar has dissolved, boil rapidly and stir (to prevent the jam from burning) for 2–3 minutes. Add the pectin, stir well and simmer for 2 minutes more.

Once the jam ready to set (see page 211), pour it into sterilized jars (see page 209) and seal immediately. Label, date and store in a cool dark place for up to 9 months.

If you live in a country that recommends processing preserves in a water bath for long-term storage, refer to online sources for advice.

Cherry Jam

A lovely jar of this cherry jam makes an elegant present. I like to add some vanilla to mine for extra flavour.

MAKES 4 X 250G (8-OZ) JARS

1kg (6½ cups) cherries, stoned (pitted)
Seeds from 1 vanilla pod or bean (optional)
1kg (5 cups) caster (superfine) sugar
125ml (½ cup) lemon juice

Place the cherries in a saucepan and add the vanilla, if using. Stir in the sugar and lemon juice and cook for 10–15 minutes until the sugar has dissolved. Stir occasionally to break down the fruit and give it a rustic consistency.

Increase the heat and bring to a rolling boil, then simmer for 12–15 minutes until the jam is ready to set (see page 211).

Pour the jam into sterilized preserving or canning jars (see page 209) and seal immediately. Label, date and store in a cool dark place for up to 9 months.

If you live in a country that recommends processing preserves in a water bath for long-term storage, refer to online sources for advice.

JAM-MAKING TIPS

- Ensure you stir the jam often during cooking because this will prevent it from sticking to the bottom of the saucepan.

- Do not boil the jam on too high a heat, or boil it for too long, as both can cause discoloration.

- Pour the jam into jars while it is hot because the heat helps a perfect seal to occur.

- Once the jars are filled to within 1cm (½ inch) of the top, place the lids on them immediately.

Wild Damson and Apple Jelly

This is the perfect jelly to make if you've never made it before.

MAKES 3 X 250G (8-OZ) JARS

900g (2lb) Cox's Orange Pippin, Bramley or cooking apples (or 6 apples), roughly sliced (do not peel or core)
850ml (3½ cups) boiling water
2kg (4½lb) wild damsons or plums, washed
Caster (superfine) sugar (see method)

Place the apples and water in a large saucepan, bring to the boil, then reduce the heat and simmer for 10 minutes or until the fruit is soft.

Add the wild damsons and simmer until they are really soft and pulpy. This is important because they must be soft to release their pectin. Mash the mixture well with a potato masher.

Strain the pulp overnight through several layers of muslin or cheesecloth suspended over a bowl. Do not squeeze the bag or the juice will become cloudy.

Measure the juice. For each 600ml (2½ cups) of liquid, weigh out 450g (2¼ cups) of caster sugar.

Pour the juice and required sugar into a large saucepan set over a low heat and stir until the sugar has dissolved. Bring to the boil, then simmer for about 10 minutes or until the mixture reaches a temperature of 105°C (221°F).

Remove the pan from the heat and check to see if the jelly is ready to set (see page 211). Pour the hot jelly into sterilized preserving or canning jars (see page 209) and seal immediately. Label, date and store in a cool dark place for up to 9 months.

If you live in a country that recommends processing preserves in a water bath for long-term storage, refer to online sources for advice.

Red Pepper Jelly

This jelly is so versatile, it is bound to become one of your larder or pantry staples. It's perfect with a cheeseboard, great when added to salads, and it can even be a marinade for barbecue beef or chicken.

MAKES 700ML (3 CUPS)

3 red (bell) peppers, deseeded and roughly chopped
600g (3 cups) jam sugar (optional, see method)
125ml (½ cup) white vinegar
2½ tbsp lemon juice

Place the red peppers in a food processor and blitz into a purée. Transfer them to a large stainless steel saucepan and add the jam sugar, vinegar and lemon juice. Bring to the boil, stirring constantly to avoid scorching, and simmer for 5–8 minutes. (If not using jam sugar, bring to a rolling boil, then add 600g/3 cups caster (superfine) sugar with 85ml/3oz liquid pectin and boil hard, stirring, for 1 minute.)

Remove the pan from the heat and leave to cool for about 15 minutes. This allows the peppers to cook slowly in the residual heat and prevents them from floating on the surface of the finished jelly.

Pour into warm, sterilized preserving or canning jars (see page 209) and seal immediately. Label, date and store in a cool dark place for 3–5 months.

If you live in a country that recommends processing preserves in a water bath for long-term storage, refer to online sources for advice.

Crab Apple Jelly

Every autumn we look forward to harvesting crab apples from Dunbrody orchard. With their sour flavour, they make a fantastic jelly that can be used for both savoury and sweet dishes.

MAKES 4 X 250G (8-OZ) JARS

2kg (4lb 8oz) crab apples, halved
Caster (superfine) sugar (see method)
Juice of 1 lemon
1 vanilla pod or bean

Place the crab apples in a large saucepan and add just enough water to cover the apples. Bring to the boil, then simmer for 20–30 minutes until the fruit softens. Do not overcook because that will destroy the pectin, which is an important setting agent.

Strain the pulp overnight through several layers of muslin or cheesecloth suspended over a bowl. Do not squeeze the bag or the juice will become cloudy.

Measure the juice. For each 600ml (2½ cups) of liquid, add 450–500g (2¼–2½ cups) of caster sugar.

Pour the juice and required sugar into a saucepan, add the lemon juice and vanilla pod, then bring the mixture to the boil, stirring to dissolve the sugar.

Keep the mixture at a rolling boil for 30–40 minutes, skimming off the froth from time to time. It is ready for bottling when it sets on the back of a chilled spoon.

Pour the jelly into warmed, sterilized preserving or jars (see page 209) and seal immediately. Label, date and store in a cool dark place for up to 6 months.

If you live in a country that recommends processing preserves in a water bath for long-term storage, refer to online sources for advice.

Red Onion Marmalade

This is a delicious commodity to have in your refrigerator. It is fantastic served with either hot or cold meat, and I sometimes use it on top of puff pastry discs topped with goats' cheese and baked in the oven. You could also use it as a topping for savoury bread, or stir it into mashed potato for a delicious caramelized flavour.

MAKES 200G (⅔ CUP)

1 tbsp rapeseed (canola) oil
4 red onions, thinly sliced
4 tbsp brown sugar
200ml (1 cup) red wine
4 tbsp red wine vinegar

Heat the rapeseed oil in a frying pan over a moderate heat. Add the onion and sauté until nicely browned, then the brown sugar and allow it to caramelize. Pour in the red wine and vinegar and reduce the mixture to a sticky consistency.

Transfer the marmalade to sterilized jars (see page 209) and seal immediately. Label, date and store in a cool dark place or the refrigerator for 6–8 weeks. Once openered, it will keep in the refrigerator for up to a week.

Kevin's Mustard Pickle

This tasty pickle is the perfect combination of sweet and savoury in a jar. It makes a wonderful accompaniment to cold meats.

MAKES 6–8 X 250G (8-OZ) JARS

½ head of cauliflower, broken into florets
2 courgettes (zucchini), cut into bite-sized chunks
1 cucumber, cut into bite-sized chunks
250g (2 cups) green beans, cut into 2cm (¾-inch) pieces
1 onion, cut into quarters
Pinch of salt
500ml (2 cups) white wine vinegar
60g (⅓ cup) sultanas (golden raisins)
5 sprigs of tarragon
150g (¾ cup) caster (superfine) sugar
3 tbsp plain (all-purpose) flour
1½ tbsp English mustard
2 tbsp ground turmeric
2¼ tbsp ground ginger

Mix the cauliflower, courgettes, cucumber, beans and onion in a large bowl and sprinkle with the salt. Cover with water and set aside overnight.

Drain off the water, then place the vegetables in a saucepan with most of the vinegar and simmer until just tender. Now add the sultanas and tarragon.

Put all the dry ingredients in a bowl and mix with the remaining vinegar to create a paste. Stir this into the vegetables over a moderate heat for about 10 minutes until the sauce has thickened.

Spoon the pickle into warmed, sterilized jars (see page 209) and seal immediately. Label, date and store in a cool dark place until required.

If you live in a country that recommends processing preserves in a water bath for long-term storage, refer to online sources for advice.

Caramelized Apple Chutney

Making this chutney is a great way of using up a glut of apples. It is very tasty with either hot or cold meats or a cheeseboard.

MAKES 6–8 X 250G (8-OZ) JARS

8 cooking apples, peeled, cored and chopped
1 onion, finely chopped
4 garlic cloves, crushed
Juice of 1 lemon
300ml (1¼ cups) white wine vinegar (or use cider or malt vinegar)
200g (1⅓ cups) raisins
1 tbsp ground ginger
2 tsp salt
400g (2 cups) soft brown sugar

Put the apple, onion, garlic, lemon juice and 200ml (1 cup) of the vinegar in a large saucepan and bring to the boil. Add the raisins, ground ginger, salt, sugar and the remaining vinegar and simmer over a very low heat for 1 hour until nicely thickened. If required, simmer for a further 30 minutes until thick.

Pour the chutney into clean, sterilized preserving or canning jars (see page 209) and seal immediately. Label, date and store in a cool dark place for 6–8 weeks months.

If you live in a country that recommends processing preserves in a water bath for long-term storage, refer to online sources for advice.

Cranberry and Orange Relish

You will never again return to shop-bought cranberry sauce after tasting this relish. It makes the perfect Christmas gift for friends too.

MAKES 250G (8OZ)

250g (2½ cups) fresh cranberries
115g (⅔ cup) caster (superfine) sugar
Grated rind and juice of 1 orange
4 tbsp water
2 tbsp port
1 cinnamon stick

Place all the ingredients in a saucepan, bring to the boil, then simmer for 8–10 minutes until the cranberries have 'popped'. Remove the cinnamon stick, then transfer the relish to sterilized preserving or canning jars (see page 209) and seal immediately. Label, date and store in a cool dark place for up to 9 months.

If you live in a country that recommends processing preserves in a water bath for long-term storage, refer to online sources for advice.

Beef Stock

There is nothing like a well-made beef stock. It is delicious in gravies, soups and sauces, and I particularly love it in French onion soup.

MAKES ABOUT 2 LITRES (8½ CUPS)

1 kg (2¼lb) beef bones
3 large carrots, roughly chopped
2 celery sticks, roughly chopped
1 onion, roughly chopped
2 bay leaves
3 sprigs of rosemary
3 sprigs of flat leaf parsley

Preheat the oven to 180°C/350°F/gas mark 4.

Place the beef bones in a large roasting pan and bake for up to 1 hour until the bones are well browned.

Transfer the bones to a large saucepan, add in the carrots, celery, onion, bay leaves and herbs and cover with water. Bring to the boil, then simmer for 2 hours, skimming the surface every so often.

Strain the stock through a fine sieve or strainer and allow to cool (preferably overnight). The next morning you can simply lift off and discard the fat, which will have solidified on the top.

Cover with clingfilm (plastic wrap) and store in the refrigerator and use within 2 days, or freeze and use within 2 months.

Chicken Stock

While this is a fantastic basic stock, if you'd like a stronger jellied stock, boil the strained stock until reduced by half. Freeze it in ice cube trays and transfer it to freezer bags for storage.

MAKES ABOUT 2 LITRES (8½ CUPS)

2kg (4½lb) chicken thighs, wings or raw carcasses, roughly chopped
2–3 sprigs each of thyme, tarragon and oregano
4 litres (17 cups) water
2 onions, roughly chopped
2 leeks, trimmed and roughly chopped
2 celery sticks, roughly chopped
2 carrots, roughly chopped
½ garlic bulb, unpeeled
2 tsp sea salt

Preheat the oven to 200°C/400°F/gas mark 6.

Place the chicken pieces or carcasses in a large roasting pan and roast for 15–20 minutes, turning them once or twice, until dark golden in colour.

Transfer the bones to a stockpot or large saucepan with the herbs. Pour over the water and bring to the boil, using a spoon to skim off any scum that rises to the surface.

Add the onions, leeks, celery and carrots to the pan with the garlic and salt. Return to the boil, then simmer, uncovered, for about 3 hours, skimming occasionally.

Taste the stock to check the seasoning and adjust as necessary. When you are happy with it, remove from the heat and strain the stock through a muslin- or cheesecloth-lined colander into a large jug or bowl, discarding the bones, vegetables and herbs. Leave to cool, then cover with clingfilm (plastic wrap) and store in the refrigerator and use within 2 days, or freeze and use within 2 months.

Fish Stock

Here's a great fish stock for use in soups. For a more concentrated flavour to use as the base for sauces, reduce the strained stock by half again. Freeze it in ice cube trays and transfer the cubes to freezer bags for storage.

MAKES ABOUT 2 LITRES (8½ CUPS)

2 onions, chopped
1 leek, trimmed and roughly chopped
1 carrot, chopped
1 celery stick, chopped
2 garlic cloves, unpeeled
100ml (½ cup) olive oil
1.5kg (3¼lb) white fish bones and heads, well
   rinsed and roughly chopped
2 litres (8½ cups) water
2 sprigs each of tarragon, flat leaf parsley and
   thyme, tied together with kitchen string
½ lemon, sliced
Salt and black pepper

Place the onions, leek, carrot, celery and garlic in a stockpot or large saucepan. Add the oil and heat until the vegetables start to sizzle. Cover and gently sweat the vegetables over a low heat for about 15 minutes until softened but not coloured.

Add the fish bones and heads to the pan and pour in the water. Stir in the herbs, lemon and seasoning. Bring to the boil, skimming off any scum that rises to the surface, then simmer, uncovered, for 20 minutes – no longer, or the bones will become bitter. Set the pan aside for at least 10 minutes to allow the flavours to infuse.

Strain the stock through a muslin- or cheesecloth-lined colander into a large jug or bowl, discarding the bones, vegetables and herbs. Leave to cool, then cover with clingfilm (plastic wrap) and store in the refrigerator and use within 2 days, or freeze and use within 2 months.

Vegetable Stock

Try adding a splash of wine for a more intense flavour.

MAKES ABOUT 2 LITRES (8½ CUPS)

3 onions, roughly chopped
1 leek, trimmed and roughly chopped
2 celery sticks, roughly chopped
1 garlic bulb, halved
6 carrots, roughly chopped
¼ tsp white peppercorns
¼ tsp black peppercorns
1 small bay leaf
2–3 sprigs each of basil, fresh coriander (cilantro),
   thyme, flat leaf parsley and tarragon, tied
   together with kitchen string
Pinch of salt
2 litres (8½ cups) water

Place the onions, leek, celery, garlic and carrots in a stockpot or large saucepan. Add the peppercorns and herbs, and season with the salt. Pour in the water and bring to the boil, then simmer for 10 minutes.

Set aside until completely cold, then transfer it to a large jug or bowl. Cover with clingfilm (plastic wrap) and chill in the refrigerator for 24 hours.

Strain the stock through a muslin- or cheesecloth-lined colander into a large jug or bowl, discarding the vegetables, peppercorns and herbs. Leave to cool, then cover with clingfilm (plastic wrap) and store in the refrigerator and use within 2 days, or freeze and use within 2 months.

Index

A

ale: pale ale and cheddar soup 25
almonds: courgette and almond
    soup 18
apples
    apple and blackberry marmalade
        crumble 192
    apple compote 114
    caramelized apple chutney 217
    simple apple tart 186
    spiced apple jellies 178
    white pudding, cheese and
        caramelized apple tarts 123
    wild damson and apple jelly 214
Arthurstown fish chowder 22
arugula *see* rocket
asparagus
    asparagus, Cratloe sheep's cheese
        and orzo risotto 126
    chicken fricassé with crushed
        baby potatoes and asparagus 72

B

bacon
    Ardrahan cheese, potato and
        smoked bacon gratin 122
    dandelion salad with bacon and
        poached egg 120
    Kilmore Quay mussels with bacon
        and white wine 60
    pheasant and bacon casserole 82
    potato and bacon soup 17
    trout fillets with streaky bacon 50
banana and berry smoothie 190
basil oil 209
beef
    beef and Guinness pie 95
    beef stock 218
    bookmaker's sandwich 105
    flank steak with confit shallots
        105
    Kevin's classic beef burger 100
    Mum's meatloaf 104
    pan-seared fillet of beef with a
        lively Cashel Blue cheese salad
        98
    pulled corned beef 92
    rib of beef with baby onions and
        horseradish cream 94
    roasted garlic cottage pie 96
beetroot and baby potato salad 140
beets *see* beetroot

berry compote 170–1
beurre noisette, skate with 49
biscuits: orange cream 201
    wine 201
blackberries
    apple and blackberry marmalade
        crumble 192
    blackberry jam 211
blackcurrants
    blackcurrant jus 86
    blackcurrant sauce 46
bookmaker's sandwich 105
boulangère potatoes 162
bread 26–39
    bookmaker's sandwich 105
    bread sauce 206
    buttermilk scones 31
    caramelized onion 36
    corkscrew 34
    oatmeal soda 30
    potato 38
    sourdough 32–3
    traditional brown soda 28
    Waterford blaa 35
bread and butter pudding, croissant
    194
broths
    cure-all chicken 21
    pulled corned beef 92
Brussels sprouts with chestnuts
    and cranberries 151
buttermilk
    buttermilk and heather-infused
        panna cotta 174
    buttermilk scones 31
butternut squash: roasted
    butternut squash mousseline 150

C

cabbage
    pickled sweet and sour red
        cabbage 146
    spring cabbage soup 12
cakes
    lemon curd sponge with
        strawberries 197
    porter cake lollies 200
carrots
    carrot and cumin purée 86
    sweet and sour 150
casseroles
    blind Irish stew 133

pheasant and bacon 82
cauliflower, pea and potato curry
    129
celeriac Waldorf salad 144
champ 157
cheese
    Ardrahan cheese, potato and
        smoked bacon gratin 122
    asparagus, Cratloe sheep's cheese
        and orzo risotto 126
    baby leek gratin with smoked
        Gubbeen 154
    baked eggs with spinach 137
    Cashel Blue cheese salad 98
    cheesy croutons 13
    pale ale and cheddar soup 25
    pancetta and cheese mash 159
    spinach and goats' cheese filo
        pastry pie 132
    white pudding, cheese and
        caramelized apple tarts 123
    see also cream cheese
cherries
    cherry jam 213
    cherry tiramisu 196
    Skeaghanore duck breasts with
        black cherries 84
chestnuts
    Brussels sprouts with
        cranberries and 151
    chestnut, cranberry and
        sausagemeat stuffing 152
chicken
    chicken and ham pie 74
    chicken fricassé 72
    chorizo roast 70
    crispy braised chicken thighs with
        chicory, olives and lemon rind
        73
    cure-all chicken broth 21
    smoked chicken terrine 76
    sticky glaze chicken thighs with
        Asian stuffing 68–9
    stock 218
chicory, crispy braised chicken
    thighs with 73
chips, thick hand-cut 165
chive mash 159
chocolate
    chocolate cream 176
    trio of chocolate fondues 177
chorizo roast chicken 70

chowder, Arthurstown fish 22
Christmas turkey, Kevin's 80
chutney, caramelized apple 217
clams: ragout of clams and cod 57
Colcannon mash 158
compotes
  apple 114
  berry 170–1
confit
  confit of duck leg 86
  confit shallots 105
Connemara air-dried lamb and garlic tart 112
consomme, wild strawberry 172
cookies see biscuits
corkscrew bread 34
courgettes
  courgette and almond soup 18
  courgette gratin 156
  courgette tagliatelli 128
crab apple jelly 214
cranberries
  Brussels sprouts with chestnuts and 151
  chestnut, cranberry and sausagemeat stuffing 152
  cranberry and orange relish 217
  cranberry jus 87
cream cheese
  orange cream biscuits 201
  smoked salmon gateaux 64
crème Anglaise 210
crisps
  curried parsnip 88
  game 165
croissant bread and butter pudding 194
crumble, apple and blackberry marmalade 192
cure-all chicken broth 21
curries
  cauliflower, pea and potato 129
  curried mussel soup 24
  curried parsnip crisps 88
  curried parsnip soup 16

D
damsons: wild damson and apple jelly 214
dandelion salad with bacon and poached egg 120
dauphinoise potatoes 162
devilled Dublin Bay prawns 56
dressings: Dalkey mustard 207
  vinaigrette 120

drinks
  indulgent eggnog 193
  smoothies 190
duck
  confit of duck leg with carrot and cumin purée and blackcurrant jus 86
  pan-seared mallard with a crunchy walnut stuffing 83
  Skeaghanore duck breasts with black cherries 84
dulse potatoes 163
Duncannon smoked fish pie 58
Dunmore East fresh scallop tartlets 62

E
eggs
  baked eggs with spinach 137
  dandelion salad with bacon and poached egg 120
  indulgent eggnog 193
elderflower and gooseberry fool 184
endive see chicory
Eton mess, kinky 180

F
fig and orange salad 78
fish 40–65
  Arthurstown fish chowder 22
  Duncannon smoked fish pie 58
  fish stock 219
  pan-fried halibut with samphire 53
  pike with vinegar and crushed peppercorns 52
  ragout of clams and cod 57
  skate with beurre noisette 49
  smoked salmon gateaux 64
  smoked Slade mackerel fillets with blackcurrant sauce 46
  sole with capers and lemon sauce 48
  trout fillets with streaky bacon and flaked almonds 50
  whole roasted sea bass in a sea salt crust 54
  whole salmon baked in a smouldering pit 44
fondues, trio of chocolate 177
fool, elderflower and gooseberry 184

G
game 82–9
game crisps 165

garlic
  cherry tomato and roasted garlic soup 14
  Connemara air-dried lamb and garlic tart 112
  garlic mash 96, 104
  roasted garlic cottage pie 96
  sautéed garlic potatoes 160
  wild garlic pesto 208
gateaux, smoked salmon 64
gelato, frozen yogurt 170–1
goats' cheese
  baked eggs with spinach 137
  spinach and goats' cheese filo pastry pie 132
gooseberry fool, elderflower and 184
grape jam, rhubarb 212
gratins
  Ardrahan cheese, potato and smoked bacon 122
  baby leek 154
  courgette 156
Guinness: beef and Guinness pie 95

H
ham
  chicken and ham pie 74
  watercress, ham and crème fraîche soup 20
  whole glazed ham 116
horseradish cream 94

I
Irish stew, blind 133

J
jam
  blackberry 211
  cherry 213
  rhubarb and grape 212
jellies
  crab apple 214
  raspberry and oolong tea 173
  red pepper 214
  spiced apple 178
  wild damson and apple 214
jus
  blackcurrant 86
  cranberry 87

K
Kilmore Quay mussels with bacon and white wine 60

L

lamb
  braised lamb shanks with
    cannellini beans 108
  Connemara air-dried lamb and
    garlic tart 112
  lamb sweetbreads with shiitake
    and broad beans 113
  roast leg of lamb with red wine
    reduction 106
  slow-roasted shoulder of Wexford
    lamb 109
  Wexford rack of lamb with Asian
    spices 110
langoustines *see* prawns
leeks: baby leek gratin 154
lemons
  crispy braised chicken thighs with
    chicory, olives and lemon rind
    73
  kinky Eton mess 180
  lemon curd sponge with
    strawberries 197
  lemon-cured pork belly 118–19
  lemon mousse with candied zest
    182
  sole with capers and lemon sauce
    48
lobster: oven-baked lobster with
  Dalkey mustard cream sauce 42

M

marmalade
  apple and blackberry marmalade
    crumble 192
  orange Irish whiskey 211
  red onion 215
marshmallow skewers, peach and
  188
meat 90–123
meatloaf, Mum's 104
meringue: kinky Eton mess 180
mint
  garden pea and mint soup 10
  mint sauce 206
mousse
  lemon mousse with candied zest
    182
  yogurt 178
mousseline, roasted butternut
  squash 150
mushrooms, pickled forest 148
mussels
  Arthurstown fish chowder 22
  curried mussel soup 24

Kilmore Quay mussels with bacon
  and white wine 60
mustard
  Dalkey mustard cream sauce 42
  Dalkey mustard dressing 207
  Kevin's mustard pickle 216

O

oats
  oatmeal soda bread 30
  traditional brown soda bread 28
oil, basil 209
onions
  boulangère potatoes 162
  caramelized onion bread 36
  caramelized onion soup 13
  red onion marmalade 215
  sage and onion stuffing 152
oolong tea: raspberry and oolong
  tea jellies 173
oranges
  cranberry and orange relish 217
  fig and orange salad 78
  orange cream biscuits 201
  orange Irish whiskey marmalade
    211
  orange pudding 198
oxtail open ravioli 102–3

P

pancetta and cheese mash 159
panna cotta, buttermilk and
  heather-infused 174
parsnips: curried parsnip crisps 88
  curried parsnip soup 16
passion fruit and honey yogurt 173
pasta
  asparagus, Cratloe sheep cheese
    and orzo risotto 126
  courgette tagliatelli 128
  oxtail open ravioli 102–3
peach and marshmallow skewers
  188
pearl barley: blind Irish stew 133
peas
  cauliflower, pea and potato curry
    129
  garden pea and mint soup 10
peppers: red pepper jelly 214
pesto, wild garlic 208
pheasant and bacon casserole 82
pickles
  Kevin's mustard 216
  pickled forest mushrooms 148
  pickled sweet and sour red
    cabbage 146

pies
  beef and Guinness 95
  chicken and ham 74
  puff pastry potato 134
  spinach and goats' cheese 132
pigeon: wood pigeon salad 88
plums: red wine and plum
  reduction 83
pork
  lemon-cured pork belly 118–19
  roast pork with crunchy crackling
    114
porter cake lollies 200
potatoes
  Ardrahan cheese, potato and
    smoked bacon gratin 122
  beetroot and baby potato salad
    140
  boulangère 162
  cauliflower, pea and potato curry
    129
  champ 157
  chicken fricassée with crushed
    baby potatoes 72
  chive mash 159
  Colcannon mash 158
  crushed baby potatoes 166
  dauphinoise potatoes 162
  dulse potatoes 163
  Duncannon smoked fish pie 58
  game crisps 165
  garlic mash 96, 104
  hasselback potatoes 166
  Mum's roast potatoes 164
  pancetta and cheese mash 159
  potato and bacon soup 17
  potato bread 38
  potato rösti 160
  puff pastry potato pie 134
  sautéed garlic potatoes 160
  thick hand-cut chips 165
poultry 66–81
prawns
  Arthurstown fish chowder 22
  devilled Dublin Bay prawns 56

R

ragout of clams and cod 57
raspberries
  kinky Eton mess 180
  raspberry and oolong tea jellies
    173
relish, cranberry and orange 217
rhubarb and grape jam 212
rice pudding: vanilla rice pudding
  and chocolate cream 176

risotto, asparagus, Cratloe sheep's cheese and orzo 126
rocket: simple rocket salad 144
rosemary: slow-roasted shoulder of Wexford lamb with 109

S
sage and onion stuffing 152
salads 138–45
    beetroot and baby potato 140
    celeriac Waldorf 144
    dandelion salad with bacon and poached egg 120
    fig and orange 78
    lively Cashel Blue cheese 98
    samphire 142
    simple rocket 144
    wood pigeon 88
samphire
    pan-fried halibut with samphire 53
    samphire salad 142
sandwiches, bookmaker's 105
sauces
    béchamel 204
    blackcurrant 46
    bread 206
    butterscotch 188, 210
    capers and lemon 48
    crème Anglaise 210
    Dalkey mustard cream 42
    hollandaise 205
    mint 206
    tarragon butter 204
    turkey gravy 207
sausagemeat: chestnut, cranberry and sausagemeat stuffing 152
scallops: Dunmore East fresh scallop tartlets 62
scones, buttermilk 31
sea asparagus see samphire
seaweed: dulse potatoes 163
shallots
    blind Irish stew 133
    confit shallots 105
sheep's cheese: asparagus, Cratloe sheep's cheese and orzo risotto 126
shittake mushrooms: lamb sweetbreads with shiitake and broad beans 113
Skeaghanore duck breasts with black cherries 84
smoothies
    banana and berry 190

Harvey Wallbanger's 190
soda bread
    oatmeal 30
    traditional brown 28
soups 8–25
    Arthurstown fish chowder 22
    caramelized onion 13
    cherry tomato and roasted garlic 14
    courgette and almond 18
    cure-all chicken broth 21
    curried mussel 24
    curried parsnip 16
    garden pea and mint 10
    pale ale and cheddar 25
    potato and bacon 17
    spring cabbage 12
    watercress, ham and crème fraîche 20
sourdough bread 32–3
spiced apple jellies 178
spinach
    baked eggs with spinach 137
    spinach and goats' cheese filo pastry pie 132
spring cabbage soup 12
stew see casseroles
stock 218–19
strawberries
    banana with berry smoothie 190
    kinky Eton mess 180
    lemon curd sponge with strawberries 197
    wild strawberry consommé 172
stuffing
    Asian 68–9
    chestnut, cranberry and sausagemeat 152
    crunchy walnut 83
    sage and onion 152

T
tarragon butter sauce 204
tarts
    cherry tomato tarte tatin 130
    Connemara air-dried lamb and garlic 112
    Dunmore East fresh scallop tartlets 62
    simple apple 186
    white pudding, cheese and caramelized apple 123
terrine, smoked chicken 76
tomatoes
    cherry tomato and roasted garlic soup 14

cherry tomato tarte tatin 130
devilled Dublin Bay prawns 56
ragout of clams and cod 57
turkey:
    Kevin's Christmas 80
    smoked turkey with fig and orange salad 78
    turkey gravy 207

V
vanilla
    crème Anglaise 210
    Harvey Wallbanger's smoothie with vanilla float 190
    vanilla rice pudding and chocolate cream 176
vegetables
    stock 219
    see also individual types of vegetable
vegetarian dishes 124–37
venison: fillet of venison poached in mulled wine 87

W
walnuts
    celeriac Waldorf salad 144
    crunchy walnut stuffing 83
watercress, ham and crème fraîche soup 20
Waterford blaa 35
white pudding, cheese and caramelized apple tarts 123
wild garlic pesto 208
wine
    fillet of venison poached in mulled wine with a cranberry jus 87
    Kilmore Quay mussels with bacon and white wine 60
    red wine and plum reduction 83
    wine biscuits 201
wood pigeon salad with curried parsnip crisps 88

Y
yeast 34
yogurt
    frozen yogurt gelato with berry compote 170–1
    passion fruit and honey yogurt 173
    yogurt mousse 178

Z
zucchini see courgettes

Acknowledgements

A new book is always a challenge, but with the support and assistance of my team at Dunbrody – particularly Julien Clémot, my Development Chef, and Niamh Donegan, my Personal Assistant, who both endured long hours and many tastings – the end result was everything I hoped to achieve.

Thank you to the team at Octopus Publishing Group: Denise Bates for believing in the book and commissioning it; Clare Churly for her extraordinary efforts and assistance, an absolute pleasure to work with; Juliette Norsworthy for her exceptional design and attention to detail; Caroline Alberti for managing the production of this book on such a tight schedule; Kate Blinman, the home economist, who emulated my style and was a true pleasure to work with; and last, but by no means least, thanks to Cristian Barnett, the photographer, for the stunning photography throughout the book.

Thanks also to the team at RTÉ Cork, especially Colm Crowley, Marie Toft and Caoimhe Buckley-Greene for coordinating the book tie-in; Barry Donnellan for keeping me on the straight and narrow for the duration of filming here at Dunbrody; and to all the team for their assistance in filming the series to accompany this book!

None of this would have been possible without the hard work of my agent Martine Carter or Brandon Evans, my US Manager, whose hard work and commitment brought the show to America.